Charles Colbeck

On the Teaching of Modern Languages in Theory and Practice

Charles Colbeck

On the Teaching of Modern Languages in Theory and Practice

ISBN/EAN: 9783743338531

Manufactured in Europe, USA, Canada, Australia, Japa

Cover: Foto ©Lupo / pixelio.de

Manufactured and distributed by brebook publishing software (www.brebook.com)

Charles Colbeck

On the Teaching of Modern Languages in Theory and Practice

PREFACE.

THESE Lectures were written at the request of the Teachers' Training Syndicate. The second appears in a slightly altered form. As delivered it consisted largely of oral illustrations and comments, only a portion of which is now printed, while some parts have been expanded. There seems to be at last a disposition to regard seriously the pretensions of Modern Languages to a larger place in Education, and I am not therefore without hope that the First Lecture, if only by the criticism which it evokes, may in some way serve to promote their claim, and especially their claim as Literature, to a fair hearing. Teachers generally find details concerning the practice of other teachers interesting, but I can not flatter myself that any one else will read the Second Lecture to the end.

My grateful acknowledgments are due to Mr R. H. Quick for help and counsel in old days and again upon this occasion, and to my colleague Mr W. G. Guillemard, to whom I owe in particular the piece of German Prose given as a model in the Second Lecture and who generously placed his note-books at my disposal.

C. C.

Harrow, May, 1887.

LECTURE I.

ON THE TEACHING OF MODERN LANGUAGES.

I.

I MUST begin by stating that Modern Languages in these lectures mean the languages and literatures of France and Germany. Not that I am so rash or so wholly ignorant as to think that no other modern language has a claim to rank beside these, or that I wish to be so rigidly practical that I would exclude all considerations of what, not is, but ought to be the actual state of the case; but because whatever I may have to say from my own experience and knowledge necessarily applies to these two alone, for I know no others—and have taught no others. Nor do I include English, for the teaching of the mother tongue, though the reasons for it are in many cases the same, is in practice so different from the teaching of a foreign language that the two cannot profitably be considered together.

Nor again, except incidentally, do I intend to put forward any opinions upon the kind of teaching which will be proper for your Professors of Modern Languages when you possess them, nor upon your happily inaugurated Modern Languages

Tripos, though this latter bears most materially upon the school teaching of the future and cannot therefore be wholly excluded.

If I begin then, as I shall, by asking "Why do we teach French and German at all?" it is because upon our answer will depend the method upon which we proceed in teaching them. Or rather the method *should* depend upon this; but alas! method is apt to be merely traditional; and Societies and Syndicates for the training of Teachers have done no service more real in the cause of education than by impressing even upon the unwilling minds of those who believe that there is no science of education at all, but only at most an art, and that an art without a theory, the necessity of considering what portion of their daily practice really serves the end which they are seeking.

Why then do we teach Modern Languages?

Essentially because they are so supremely useful. Let us not be ashamed to say this. The advance in the teaching of them has kept pace and will continue to keep pace with the advance of utilitarianism in education; nay the very doctrine on which their claims are based was formulated just about the time when French first obtained a place in the regular course of instruction in our English public schools. Sixty years ago, I do not believe that any public school taught French except as an extra, like drawing and dancing, and I do not believe that any taught German at all. A liberal education was an education for a class born into a world of already secured positions, a world of sinecurists and courtiers, of place-holders and pluralists, of broad acres and fat livings, a world therefore for which the traditionary classics were all-sufficient, and whose ideal, no ignoble one withal,—for I do not mean, or think or allege

that the education was a bad one, I only say that it made
no provision for a work-a-day world,—whose ideal was
summed up in the time-honoured phrase "a scholar and a
gentleman". But the world outside the schools was widening.
Science was already knocking at their doors. Commerce
and industry, travel and geography, the inclusion in the
public school system of the middle classes, the increase of
population, the reform of the public services, competitive
examinations, the Napoleonic wars, the writings of Goethe
and Schiller, a German Prince Consort, international exhibitions, international trade, the struggle for existence and
survival of the fittest, these and all that they implied
combined to raise the study of modern languages from the
status of an accomplishment, or a commercial art, on a
level let us say with book-keeping, to rank as an integral
portion of a liberal education. Those who had to devise
examinations for the public services could not but consider the matter from the utilitarian stand-point, though
deference to tradition—and especially to the tradition of
fashion, that worst of all traditions, in as much as it substitutes servility for veneration—largely interfered with
their work. Still we can see that at the basis of our
competitive examinations is the one principle which can
never lead us astray; that education means the training of
a man to bear himself worthily, and to perform ably his
share of the world's work; and that while much of education
will therefore be common to all, just as the qualities which
make up the worthy and able man in whatever capacity are
largely the same, yet a considerable portion of the training
of the man must depend upon the nature of the post he is
intended to occupy. And it is one not the least of the
honours of Cambridge that it has recognised that whatever

study the world needs a University should teach in all its breadth and fulness.

All studies are good for man, some more some less, some for this man some for that, and the more widely and more deeply a study is pursued, the better for the world; this it is that our Alma Mater has proclaimed aloud by her new Triposes, and nothing less than this is the true conception of a Universitas Studiorum. There is some trace still of the old mistrust, I fear I must say of the old contempt. The living languages, we have been told, are too trivial to be scholarly, too easy to be learned, too useful to be dignified. There is no language like a dead one I suppose, all else is dialect. And on the principle that to rail is not only easier than to reason, but far more attractive and persuasive to those whose interests are feeble, and who love to have their opinions formed for them, a Modern Languages Tripos was dubbed a "Courier" Tripos, the Antiquarians triumphed, and what Cambridge possesses at the present moment would more properly be styled the Mediaeval and Modern Languages Tripos. Now there is everything to be said for a Mediaeval Languages Tripos in itself, though the arguments for it are not of precisely the same kind as those which make for the Modern Languages; but I venture to think that there is very little to be said for and very much to be said against this linking of the two, and in the interests of literature in general I hope that they may soon be dissociated. But I will come back to my immediate topic.

We teach Modern Languages, firstly because they are so supremely useful. If I spend a few moments in stating fully in what various ways they are so, it is because each use they serve bears upon the methods of their study.

1. Consider how a knowledge of French and German doubles and trebles, and more, the library whence knowledge may be drawn. How much of history and philosophy, of geography and travel is written in French; how much of history, of philosophy, of science, of mathematics, of geography in German! Nor can we accept the reply that all that is worth reading either has been or can be translated, for not only will translations not pay for much that is most deserving of perusal, but also translations cannot keep pace with the ever increasing mass of literature; and even if it could, it is a wasteful process, wasting in sheer superfluity the capital and labour of translator and publisher. And even so again we need a large army of translators, and these must be well trained.

2. They are useful and indispensable to the passing traveller, that is to everyone now-a-days.

3. All Europe and the coasts of the Mediterranean are no longer strange places, but a home to the resident abroad who is armed with one or both of these languages.

4. Commerce needs them at home. What proportion of corresponding clerks in our City houses are English at this present moment? How gladly and profitably would nine-tenths of our middle classes exchange their little Latin and less Greek for a passable knowledge of even one Modern Language! How laboriously do they acquire them in later life after business hours, with jaded minds and at a belated age!

5. French is still the language of diplomacy. We have all read in a recent book at what disadvantage the late Earl Russell found himself for want of an adequate knowledge of it. Some of us know that the proficiency even now of the

clerks of the Foreign Office leaves much to be desired—but I need not continue.

Secondly, we teach Modern Languages because they are, by comparison, so easy that our teaching does not run to waste.

We teach boys Greek, and we have so far advanced in honesty, or frankness, that we own that nine-tenths of them learn little, forget that little soon, and never touch a Greek book when once they leave school. We defend the practice by saying that we have been "training faculty". If we told the real truth we should say that we do it for three reasons. 1. Because we know some Greek and can teach it. 2. Because fashion demands it. 3. Because we really do want to teach it to one-tenth of our boys who will do some good with it. Now so soon as we adopt a reasonable practice and take for *all* boys Latin, if possible, and one or more living languages for that linguistic training which I believe we are all agreed is an essential part of a complete education (besides being the cheapest and for most boys the most human and exhilarating and stimulating), then and not till then we shall find that we are training faculty in reality in the nine-tenths as well as the one-tenth; and also that whatever portion our pupils have grasped of vocabulary, grammar, and literature is a possession of which they will really make use, which they will really extend, which they do really appreciate, which will bear real fruit. In other words we shall have emerged from darkness to light, from the cloud-land of fancy to the terra firma of fact. Surely it is not too much to say that before we teach any subject merely to "train faculty" we ought at least to have made the circuit of all other possible subjects of study to see if we cannot find one, in which we may combine some actual knowledge with the bare power to know.

Thirdly, we teach Modern Languages for the sake of the culture which they afford.

Having put first the bread and cheese principle of real material utility, we need not nevertheless fear to claim for living tongues a potency in kindling the imagination, ennobling thought, inspiring right feeling and worthy action, charming the ear by beauty of sound and rhythm, and the reason by force or grace, or stateliness of expression, enlivening by the brilliancy of wit and the glow of humour. We need not care to dispute as to their place and precedence in these respects; I will only venture just to express my own conviction, that while I should place Greek far above French or German, I should place Latin below either. That is not the point. If the "Humanities" are contained in French and German, then there are so many other reasons for seeking our training in the "Humanities" from them that we shall be right in so doing for the majority of the young.

It often seems to me strange, when the "Classics" in the narrow sense of the word are placed educationally so far above Modern Languages, that no offset is made for the very important fact that while the masterpieces of ancient literature are essentially pagan, modern literature is, not indeed essentially, but in colour and setting, Christian. I know that it may be said that the very greatest names in Literature, old or new, are neither Pagan nor Christian, but purely human, and that for the poets Great Pan did not die as Thamus was bidden to proclaim. I know that there is nothing nobler in any literature than much of Aeschylus, of Sophocles, of Plato, of Lucretius; I admit that if the old world was sensual and coarse the new is sensuous and sensual. That is one of the sad facts of the world, that the introduction to what is most beautiful of human work is also an introduction to what is most perilous; and I will not say that the "poisonous honey" of France is not of all that is perilous the most to be dreaded. But I do say that, while barely one escapes some taint of soul from his schoolboy classics, it is possible that in all his schoolboy reading in Modern Languages he may, (and we teachers ought to see that he does), escape the introduction to anything that can fairly be called demoralizing. The *knowledge* of evil is inevitable—the virtue of the modern world is like Milton's not "fugitive or cloistered". But at least the atmosphere of modern literature is full of the ideas that the world owes to Christianity. Do you know the lines of a poet who was no saint and no preacher and would have solved the riddle of existence without revelation if he could? I mean Alfred de Musset. They are from a remarkable poem entitled 'Espoir en Dieu'. He says

"Une immense espérance a traversé la terre;
Malgré nous vers le ciel il faut lever les yeux,"

and Horace and Epicurus discourse to us in vain.

Therefore I say, Teach a boy Greek *if* you can; and if you cannot, give him, in a good translation, Homer and the Prometheus Vinctus, and the Oedipus at Colonus and the Antigone, and the end of the Phaedo, the Apology and the Crito. Their thoughts are part of his inheritance, and he must enter into possession. But give him also, *because* you can, without over-taxing even feeble powers or using hours that ought not to be spared, give him the power to read in the original such works as Faust, in which all the bitter-sweet of emotion and intellect finds manifold expression, as Wallenstein and Don Carlos, as Hermann and Dorothea, and Reineke Fuchs, as Barfüssele, most charming of a thousand charming idylls; and in French such works as the Tartuffe and a hundred more plays, as Notre Dame de Paris, as La Mare au Diable, and Consuelo, and as that most touching, to my mind, of all poems that are, because it is instinct with the wonders and terrors of the sea, with the courage and devotion that consecrate human labour, and with the pitying love that transmutes misfortune and misery into precious jewels—I mean that poem of the Légendes des Siècles entitled "Les Pauvres Gens".

Fourthly, we teach Modern Languages as a branch of science and research. I shall have a good deal to say presently as to the limitations which are advisable and necessary in this direction at school, but considering them as learned languages and considering them apart, the scholar who sets himself to learn historically the grammar, phonology, and literature of France or Germany will find as deep an interest and as wide a field as he can desire. Now the true relation of the teaching of the young to research and speciality is this—that our teaching should lead them a little way in these directions, should give to *all* a conception of what has been done for them in the past, of what still needs doing and how well worth the doing it is; to give to the *few* some small equipment for their quest.

To carry out this in German and above all in French is a useful and pleasant task.

For use in life then, for linguistic training of the mind, as culture, as science, we claim for Modern Languages the right to stand in no rank below the first, and if weighed against other subjects, to be declared of more value because of the manifold nature of the education which they can bestow.

Let me now try to state in what way the method which we shall adopt will depend upon the use which we intend to make of the languages.

For use in actual life, we all wish to be able to read them. I put that clearly first. If the two powers could be entirely separated, and we were given the choice of the power to read French or of the power to converse in it, or of the power to correspond in it, I cannot doubt that we should choose the first; though we should all gladly be able also to converse in it, and we should many of us be very glad if we could correspond in it and translate from English prose into it in good style. Fortunately, if I am right in placing our wants in that order, that is precisely the order in which they are the easiest to satisfy, and the vanity and inordinateness of human wishes for once fail to find an illustration. But it is not the order in which our knowledge naturally developes: the reading and the power of composition are linked more or less closely together, while the power to converse (easily acquired under certain conditions presently to be considered) stands apart and presents some peculiarities. Now, if reading is the most important and universal need, it follows that we shall attend to this first (unless there be some reason to suppose that conversation must be learnt very early or not at all), and we shall not therefore be as anxious as some teachers are to begin in the nursery, and to provide for all children the Swiss bilingual bonne. I should not for my own part place the study of any language but its own very early in a child's training. Observation of the world, geography, history, the elementary notions of number, form, and space, the intelligent reading and learning of the mother tongue all seem to me to have a prior claim. If our children begin at nine or ten they will go far enough before they leave school, if justice is done them. Not that if opportunity occurs for Modern Languages I regard them as harmful, or that if boys arrived at Harrow having already like M. Jourdain spoken French prose all their life without knowing it, I should wish for the mere pleasure or profit of teaching them to proceed to change the unconscious into conscious knowledge; but I do mean that the usual school method of beginning by setting a boy to learn his grammar and as soon as may be to read a book, is only so far wrong that *I* would begin by helping him to read a book and letting him as soon as may be learn his grammar.

And here, "impar congressus Achilli", I must perforce break a lance with the Master of Balliol even at the risk of extermination without being allowed appeal à miséricorde. You have all seen at least a brief report of his charming speech in welcome to the Professeurs de Français at Oxford, and I hope you have all seen it reported at length. He places the Modern Languages as high as I would; he expresses with force and grace all the dignity of the literature of France; he rises high, as one would expect, above the fetish worship of the Classics, and he would insist on a knowledge of a Modern Language as a necessary and indispensable qualification for admission to a University. But he thinks Modern Languages can be taught between the ages of six and ten, and not one language only but two, and even a third! and he thinks the linguistic faculty is strongest at ten and extinct at twenty.

"The first step towards a more successful study of Modern Languages is to teach them in the order and manner which nature indicates. We observe that while the powers of the mind usually strengthen as years advance, at least until the end of middle life, the faculty of learning a new language decays almost in an inverse ratio. A very few only retain this, as well as some other gifts of childhood, throughout life. But, in general, the power of acquiring languages is soon lost. It is stronger before than after ten years of age, before twenty than after twenty, and so on in the successive stages of life. The infant learns his own language in a manner which is almost mysterious to us. He makes and understands signs. He wants to speak and to be spoken to. He uses gestures to help out his own inarticulateness. The fountain of speech is rising to the surface, and he soon breaks out into words and phrases. He is always repeating the names of things and persons which he knows, and the more he can babble the better he is pleased. At five or six years of age he has a stock of at least 400 or 500 words, and a grammar of his own, which is nearly perfect, and which he rarely, if ever, violates. But the faculty of speech is not yet exhausted. If, at the age of five or six years, he is transplanted into another country, and hears French or some other language everywhere spoken, he will acquire the new language much in the same manner as he acquired the old, and with nearly equal facility; the power of imitation is alive in him still. The short period of six months is said to be enough to perfect a clever child in a new language, that is to say, within the limits of his own narrow circle of wants and ideas. The familiarity which he has thus acquired in the use and pronunciation of a language may be forgotten in after life, but is easily recovered, and he will always possess a great advantage over another, whose knowledge of French and German is acquired by reading only. To a second language, if his surroundings are again changed, the child may even add a third, which he learns in the same childish fashion. It is to be observed that he rarely confuses different languages. If the weight becomes too great for his memory, one drives out the other. They are learned as a whole and they are forgotten as a whole. But the forgotten language is still latent in his mind, and may be easily recovered—not at once, but in a very few days or weeks when the sounds which he has heard so often in childhood once more catch his ear."

The paragraph is delightful, and with much I cordially and from experience agree, but as for the linguistic power dying at twenty and decaying at ten, I can honestly say that one of the pleasantest recollections I have of much teaching of easy German is the rapidity with which an older boy, say of sixteen (suddenly transferred to the Modern Side), gallops through the elements and takes his place shortly with the best. I am convinced that the more languages a man learns the more easily each is acquired, and that age is no impediment until indeed all the faculties begin to wane together; and if you ask me how long a grown man would take to learn what the child learns in six months, I should say (under conditions as favourable) one month. Again, and this is an essential point, Professor Jowett says that nature bids us begin by conversation, begin by the gate of the ear. I really think that this is a fallacy which can be demonstrated. I submit that for all, young or old, the eye is incomparably the *swifter* gate to knowledge, and that so soon as we can use, we *do* use it and *rightly* use it in preference to, though of course not to the exclusion of, the ear. No doubt, until the child has learnt the use of that greatest of all human inventions, the written alphabet and written speech, we must perforce proceed orally. The use of the eye in language is an artificial and laborious acquisition, but once acquired it can be applied to all languages, and it is the only means of rapidly acquiring accuracy. Nor do I mean accuracy of an intricate kind only; if I did I should be liable to the objection that this is just the part of language-teaching which we schoolmasters insist upon overmuch, as no doubt we may. It is open to a ready test by all. Take a child who has acquired good nursery French, ask him to write down a sentence, or if you think that unfair, yourself write down exactly what falls from his lips—you will find no discrimination of *-ez -er -é -ais -ai -ait*. Now count the number of times these terminations occur in a page of conversation and you can form some estimate (though far below the reality) of the extent to which he is liable to error, and how many mistakes he will make in translating and in understanding what is said or read to him, so soon as he steps beyond the very meagre and not very useful range of the sentences which, learnt by ear, are to him intelligible only as wholes. I know too well how irksome is the task of eradicating these inaccuracies, how it hurts the child's pride and chafes his patience. And if you look into the matter you will see that it is a real inaccuracy of thought which bars the way to any intelligent writing of the language at all. If, on the contrary, the language is learnt when the child can read, if the new words are first sounded to him, then written *for* him, then seen by him in print, then written *by* him, then reproduced by ear and eye, you will find that progress is faster, and retentiveness greater, and that what is known is known accurately.

It is said again that if children acquire two or more languages orally in infancy they do not mix them. That is, I believe, not the case, and if it is *not*, the objection to a polyglot mayonnaise of words is real though perhaps not very serious. I can however agree heartily in the statement that a language once learnt conversationally at any age, so as to be a real instrument of thought, within a certain range is never really forgotten. It may be overlaid by other languages or other knowledges, but the palimpsest is easily revived; the birds are still in the aviary of the mind and can be recaptured; and though I cannot see in this any argument for learning a language in childhood (unless in childhood there is nothing better to be done), it is no doubt a very important and a very comforting thought for those whose visits to foreign lands have become less frequent and whose French and German have grown rusty. I would ask you who hear me whether this, or something like this, is not the process of revival. At first neither words nor sentences will come, and we say despairingly it is gone past recall; but as the old familiar sounds surround us and we pick up again first one and then another idiom, the mind regains its ready utterance, and one long bout of foreign talk, or even of reading, sends us to bed once more to find that even in our dreams our thoughts frame themselves not in English but in the foreign tongue, and we feel that we resume our progress almost at the point where we left off.

But it will be urged, the true accent is never acquired in later years, the tongue and throat are less supple, the ear less quick to note the true sounds. Now it would be strange if it were so, for in music the childish ear is less quick than in the stage of maturity, and the mother-tongue is *not* best spoken between the ages of six and eight, indeed some sounds are then impossibilities to many children. Nor is it my experience that pronunciation cannot be learned by a boy of fifteen or a man of twenty or thirty. The reason of the extremely faulty pronunciation of all schoolboys and of most of their teachers is not that they *cannot* be taught it, but that for various reasons they *are* not. I shall have something to say on this later. I will only say now that as I would rather occupy the years from six to nine or ten with other teaching than Modern Languages, so I would rather teach a child articulation, tone, and power of sustained speech and recitation through the mother tongue; and I would give a great deal of time to this much neglected side of education. There are few sounds in other languages which require the organs of speech to be used in a way in which they are not used in English. There are fewer still which are difficult of acquirement. The difficulty is not that the sound cannot be imitated, but that it is not aimed at. We visualize the letters and give them unconsciously their English force, and hence nine-tenths of our blunders.

My conclusion is therefore that the power of conversing in a foreign language can be acquired at least as easily late as early; that it is *much* less important than translation, and less important than composition, and that in learning it at whatever age we waste power if we proceed by ear only.

I do not wish to be misunderstood as holding that many children do not converse better than their elders. I do assert that when this is the case the children have, as a matter of fact, given to the acquisition of this power more time and pains than their elders would have to bestow in order to rival them, and that it would be a great pity to endeavour so to lay out a scheme of education as to bring in conversational Modern Languages at an early date. If any one doubts this let him try to estimate (1) the number of hours daily which a child living with foreigners is talking or being talked to in a foreign language, (2) the number of distinct separate efforts which have been made by the child, (3) the number of distinct instructional efforts bestowed upon the child by an individual with no one else to attend to; and then sum up the number of similar advantages which their elders with whom they are compared, as I hold so unfairly, have enjoyed during their term of learning. Of course if the child lives abroad, or the mother or nurse can teach this well and not the other subjects (in short if the case be special), I do not say the balance of gain would not be on the side of so teaching. There remains the objection often urged that memory is strongest in the child of all the faculties, and that therefore conversation, which depends chiefly on memory, can only be acquired young. But again I would answer, granting as I do grant that it depends on memory, and that memory is strong at an early age—I do not believe that it is stronger in childhood than in mature age, which is the only assumption that can justify the inference that is drawn. Memory is always, it seems to me, quite as strong as is needed, generally too strong, certainly too much insisted on, and of all the faculties the least noble. It should be the merest handmaid and severely subordinated. It is early developed, and we should be wrong to appeal too soon to reason, but with so much upon which we can exercise memory usefully let us at least make a careful selection of the tasks which we will set it. I would use it to give the child an ample store of the simpler poems of its own language, of the treasures in prose of its English Bible, of the names of the flowers of the field, of the birds of the air, and the living creatures of the world about it; I would make memory the handmaid of the equally early developed power of observation, from which so much more delight and more real mental development may be derived. I have not mentioned the difficulty of procuring good teaching for children, nor the expense, which would prevent the system ever extending below the wealthy classes and even the very wealthy classes; yet it is not for the wealthy that education will be or ought to be mainly organized.

But if I have maintained the paramount supremacy of the *eye* in learning, do not let me be thought to undervalue the *ear*. Whenever we desire to gain the power to converse, we must diligently use the *ear* and learn phrases and sentences as wholes. And it is by basing his teaching and handbooks upon the clear perception of this that Mr Prendergast has done a real service to language teaching.

I think he carries his theory much too far; under-estimates by far the amount of claim which his system makes upon time and energy, to say nothing of patience and interest: that he over-estimates the actual result, and still more the *value* of the result. But I would always speak with the greatest respect of his enthusiasm and industry, and of the value of what he happily terms "mastery of sentences," and of the development by his "variations" of the full use to which each type of sentence when mastered can be made to serve.

His system deserves to be studied in the book which he has devoted to it, "The Mastery of Languages", but most of you probably know one or more of his handbooks in which the system has been applied to French, German, Italian,

Spanish and Latin. It consists in brief of a few carefully chosen sentences taken up piece by piece, and on each fragment of each sentence are rung all the linguistic changes which the words will bear, the literal English being placed opposite to each foreign sentence. By the time the hundredth page is reached, out of fifteen sentences, each of some fifteen or twenty words, there have been formed some fifteen hundred sentences interrogative, negative, affirmative, etc., etc. All must be mastered, all must be kept up as you go forward; no other French words are to be looked at during the process. Lessons are to last ten minutes, to be not less than three per diem; the master's function is to hear and to give the right intonation and pronunciation. Then come, and not till then, tables of French inflexions and a system of "variations" which is really ingenious, and which I have had printed for the purpose of this lecture.

Diversifying Table showing the commonest English Words grouped so as to facilitate the making of VARIATIONS, *to be used as Exercises in vivâ voce composition in any language, whether ancient or modern.*

A. unless, if, whether, although, yet, but, besides, except, during, whilst, because, for, as, whereas, since, after, before, instead of, that, lest, until, upon, whenever, therefore, in, from, without, before, else, and, or.

B. I, thou, he, she, it, we, you, they; my, thy, his, her, its, our, your, their.

C. am, art, are; be; do, does, did; have, has, had; is, was, wast, were, wert; will, would, shall, should; can, could; may, might; must; ought, let.

D. being, been; bought, buying; brought, brings; calls, called; comes, came; doing, done; find, found; gave, given; going, gone; having; meets, met; makes, made; put; saw, seen; sell, sold; sends, sent; showed; stopped; taken, took; telling, told; wanted; went; procured.

E. me, thee, him, her, it, self, us, you, them, selves; my, his, her, its, our, your, their; mine, thine, hers, ours, yours, theirs; a, an, the.

F. which, who, whom; how much, how many; why; when; whither, whence, where; whose, what, how.

G. a, an, the; this, more, such, that, any, every, another, several, those, most, these, other, either, neither, some, many, few, rest; one, first, two, second, &c.

H. on, into, of, instead of, between, out of, about, beyond, over, through, near, among, below, under, towards, in, down, to, at, behind, beside, with, from, without, concerning, before, after.

I. together, often; to-day, yesterday, to-morrow; here, there; better, best; yes, no, not; back, very, next, first, away, soon, afterwards, well, ago, than.

DIRECTIONS.—Take any sentence, being an English version of a foreign one already committed to memory, and interchange the words, one at a time, with those in the groups to which they severally belong.

When the words in this list have all been mastered, proceed to diversify the sentences as in Examples I. and II. Substitute nouns for pronouns, and pronouns for nouns, at pleasure.

The auxiliary verbs ought frequently to be massed thus: *might have been*, &c.

DIVERSIFIED SENTENCES.

          c   b   c   e   d g   d   h   g   g

I.   Can you let me have a sitting-room on the first floor
h   g
for three days?

        c   b   c   e   d g   d   h   g   g

Will you let me *take* a sitting-room on the *third* floor
h   g
for *four* days?

         a b c   i   d   e   h c   b   c

II.   If I had not met your servant in the street, I should
i c   d   a   b   c   d   h
not have known that you had returned from Spain.

          a   b d   e   h   e   b   c

Although we saw her child near their house, we could
i   d   a   b   c   i   d   h
not believe that they had not started for Portugal.

Any one who knows how defective is the ordinary vocabulary in the matter of conjunctions, adverbs and prepositions, especially compound prepositions, will see the value of a means so simple of bringing the attention to bear upon them grouped separately and exhibiting each member in actual use. It is an ingenious, practical, labour-saving instrument, and as such should be known to every teacher and learner. Mr Prendergast has in fact called attention to the important difference between *matter* and *form*, and by enabling the learner to acquire certain "cadres" and shewing him how to import new matter into them he has done good work. Again, his method sets the mind at ease: it makes a certain part of the operation of speech mechanical, transfers the labour from the central conscious organ to a subsidiary unconscious automatic ganglion, and thus facilitates learning.

Now for my objections to his system.

I. The results are not commensurate with the pains required. The pupil is not qualified to converse at the end. The book forms a useful series of repetition lessons nicely graduated and is a good subsidiary. But this is rank heresy according to Mr Prendergast, who will be loved "all in all or not at all". I am myself a *corpus vile* on which experiment has been made. I have heard the French book once a week for fifteen years, and have gone as near to mastering it as any one ever has, I verily believe; but if I depended upon it for my power of making my wants known abroad, I should get a smaller percentage of them satisfied than I do now, which would be a serious matter. I admit however that not unfrequently in earlier days, with an inward chuckle, I used to frame my remarks into one of the well-known tags and sail away glibly to the end of my sentence, to the mingled pleasure and astonishment of my interlocutor at my sudden access of fluency and accuracy, who regarded me as Balaam may have regarded his ass on a celebrated occasion. I once quite cowed a German official at a post office into obsequiousness with a round shot from Prendergast.

II. The process is deadly dull, and of methods it may surely be said that none is wholly wrong but the dull one.

III. Idioms are far more isolated than Mr Prendergast will admit. You cannot pass from one to another by nice gradations. The result is that much of Mr Prendergast's French is poor and flabby.

IV. The vocabulary is very small, and Mr Prendergast

sets himself sternly against increasing it by reading a book.

V. It is illiterate, or at best unliterary.

VI. Following upon this, it affords no training in English as translation does. When you translate you are learning two languages at once.

VII. It is very hard to adapt to class teaching (except in the way I use it), yet our education must assume class teaching as its basis.

VIII. The teacher's power is wasted; his part is a poor one at best, and he cannot diverge from the dull track assigned to him. Yet the manifold influence of the teacher upon his class can hardly be set too high as a factor in the development of the young.

For these reasons we must reject Mr Prendergast's system when it claims to be a sole exclusive method.

Then there is the system of Ascham—the retranslation system—in which the whole analysis of the language is given by oral teaching upon a short carefully chosen model, and is followed up at once by the corresponding synthesis, which consists in the pupil turning his translation back into the original. Clearly Ascham and Mr Prendergast are at issue in that the one says, analyse each word first, and the other says, learn phrases as wholes and let the meaning of the parts be gradually driven home by the variations of the phrase. But both go slowly and insist on mastery. I do not doubt that pupils taught upon Ascham's system would have a very thorough knowledge in the end. No one has a more firm belief in the use of retranslation and of the *pen* in general than I have. I believe many a German has acquired the very full knowledge of English which the

Germans commonly possess by Aschamizing the "Vicar of Wakefield". For a long while too the whole of one sex and a large proportion of the other learnt their French from "Télémaque", and perhaps this may spare me further words, for you all know or have heard how dull the process was. I must pass on more quickly or these Lectures will grow into a book, and I will therefore only say that this system is not very well adapted for classes, because the pace of progress varies so greatly with the individual and that it is tedious if made the exclusive system; but that I do believe that both the performance of the dictionary and grammar part by the teacher orally, with the consequent avoidance of desperation on the one hand and misconception on the other, and the rule of thorough translation upon paper, besides the leading and original feature of the retranslation, are altogether sound and right and that a considerable part of our time should be given to teaching of this kind.

Akin to this is the *Hamiltonian* system of an interlinear translation for beginners, which has the merit of making something like Ascham's method possible while leaving the class to prepare alone (no small gain), and of relieving the tedium of dwelling on so minute a fragment of a book, by making rapid advance possible. A book based on this system is almost a necessary for beginners, in my opinion, though one test of their advance will be the time they take to reach a stage at which they can do without it.

What is called the *Robertsonian* method[1] carries this still further, adding to interlinear translation paraphrase, and to

---

[1] Boltz, "Conversation Grammar of the German Language". Asher and Co.

paraphrase parallel columns, and to parallel columns an elaborate commentary on the history and affinities of the words—this last so exhaustive that the pupil's feeling is that he understands the text very well and hopes in time to understand the explanations also. I do not know that more is given than a teacher *may* give *viva voce*, but just here lies the mistake: you cannot stereotype the living voice.

If I mention Mr Ollendorff it is only to say that his system is open to nearly all the objections that I have brought against the others, and that it furthermore makes no attempt to stint or enliven its cumbersome dulness. I know well that those who survive a course of it are very well equipped, and I admit that many of its principles are sound, but what we really want in a book is that it shall by all possible artifices lighten and vary the strain, and by all possible care lift the beggarly elements into the higher region of style and grace. "Balbus was building a wall" and his weary train must disappear from our books to be replaced by the art (which can be applied to all languages) that is shewn in Mr Sidgwick's introduction to Greek prose, and by the style shewn in M. Jules Bué's "Comparative Idioms".

It will have become evident that I am an eclectic as regards method, or at any rate as regards the methods as actually worked out in published books. Let me now try to sum up my own conclusions as to the method of beginning to teach a language. What I say will be based upon the supposition that our teaching is class teaching. But I would not modify it materially for individual instruction. Clever pupils can be taught by any method if taught individually, stupid or reluctant pupils present in their single selves many of the difficulties of a class (attention weak, retention ditto, interest flagging, variety necessary).

I would always begin with a book—even if my first lesson were conducted with the book shut, still I would give my pupil one. He can read an English book and likes it—sometimes. There is a foreign one and he is going to read that, it will be interesting too—in its way (I have said that I do not care that any child should begin to learn a foreign language before it can read). In French one or two lessons will teach the power of the letters, which should be made clear to the eye by phonetic English equivalents (as is indeed always done though for the *alphabet* alone).

In German there is no greater difficulty if the Roman alphabet be adopted, as it surely should be for beginners *and more than beginners.* The letters known (not *mastered* however as yet), the book can be begun, and with the book I would teach not the declensions, nor the article, but a verb first, and this verb or verbs "*to have*", "*to be*", and "*to see*" or "*to do*", or some simple transitive verb. These should be represented also phonetically (in brackets after each word). Only so does the eye help the ear instead of forestalling or misleading it. This can be done and is done [Blackboard, Sind—Zint], but it is not done enough. The *liaison* in French can be so exhibited, and the pupil should have a page or two of these phrases written as in use, and phonetically, in columns for practice. You cannot teach intonation or rhythm so (or at least not fully, though you can indicate accent), but I have been astonished more than once at the correct English pronunciation of a German who had literally learnt it from a pronouncing dictionary. The reason for learning the verb is this, that then, from the very first, synthesis can accompany analysis, and by this double process only is command of speed combined with accuracy and intelligence, and intellectual as opposed to memory training. And let the verbs be learnt as in Mr Quick's "Essentials of German", *i.e.* the simple type *printed* but the verb always said as a sentence meaning something, in collocation, *in situ*, alive not dead.

e.g.   J'ai un cheval, tu as un cheval etc.,
Ich habe es etc.,
Das bin ich, etc.,
Je le suis etc. (only don't too early point out that *le* is invariable, but remember that "tout vient à qui sait attendre").

That is the beginning of grammar. You may have it printed in a text-book or chromographed, or write or print it on the black board and let your boys copy it. That is detail—not altogether unimportant but of minor importance, and I pass on. As for your book or books (for I lay it down as essential that while you insist on and linger over small portions you also do something rapidly; take the mind on a tour of observation in this strange world and let it see what it has to learn), you will at first read much to them and they will read a little to you, and so you will feel your way to the simple declensions, the article, and the pronouns and the adjectives. If you ask what book shall you take, I answer, it hardly matters. The best is the most interesting, and the best is the most simple, and the best is the one you know best.

Fables are excellent if they do not obtrude their moral; prose is better than poetry, though poetry should be read too and some at least should be learned.

I have said that I would have an interlinear translation, and there is a little book which I have much used in beginning German called "Apel's German Stories", which gives this translation at the end, so that the boys can learn a lesson from it, and then say from the text. It is some years now since I have taught German to absolute beginners, but I do not desire a better book, and I make no doubt there is something similar in French. If not, publishers are enterprising and there would soon be twenty well printed, well chosen, probably well illustrated, and certainly cheap; for either modern language books pay whether good or bad, or publishers are content to labour for the public good gratuitously to the utmost extent that can be desired. There is a good collection of German stories by M. Wittich published by Williams and Norgate, but it is too expensive. I do not intend however, at any rate in this lecture, to mention books except incidentally—I wish to make clear my position as to method. And here probably I may best discuss a question which cannot be avoided—Should the teaching be mainly by English or native teachers? I will say at once that it is in my opinion a question of pros and cons, though I have also a clear opinion as to which way the balance inclines. I think that English teachers produce considerably the best results. "Vous êtes orfèvre, M. Josse" is of course an obvious retort, and I am willing that the *Société des Professeurs de Français* should make a full deduction on this score: but I will try to state fairly the two sides.

I. The native teacher makes no mistakes and we English teachers make scores.

II. We do not like to go beyond our book; nay some of us cannot go beyond our *Key!* We therefore cannot improvise, do not carry on the lesson in French or German, are shy of reading to our pupils, more shy still of conversing.

III. We do not inspire confidence of our knowledge in pupils, and they are apt to grow beyond us.

I admit therefore that we teach some things that are wrong and very many things not at all—sins of commission and of omission. On the other hand,

I. The native teacher is at best as weak in his English as we are in our French or German, and (even for conversational French) it is at least as important that the English should be correct as the French or German; and for translation it is more important, for there *is* the good French in the book, while the English has to be produced by master and scholar. If the master cannot provide the good English assuredly his boys will not.

II. The native teacher is not understood by his pupils, and he does not understand them, verbally I mean.

III. The native teacher, if he is to have the same command over, respect from, liking for and by his class, must be a man of superior calibre to an English teacher. It is not very hard for an average Englishman to learn to keep order in an average Form. It is very hard for an average native. But there is no reason to suppose that the average native teacher will be in these respects superior to the average Englishman. I here purposely understate my case. We all know it to be a fact that the temptation for an inferior man to try his hand at teaching his native tongue to foreigners is great: it is as true of Englishmen abroad as of foreigners in England.

IV. As a matter of fact the English teacher, if he takes any trouble to qualify himself for his task, finds no difficulty in bringing his pupils up to his own level of knowledge. Give him time enough and he will teach them all he knows himself and he will assuredly know more than the practical conditions permit of his pupils learning, *i.e.* he will always be well in advance of his boys and in no danger of losing self-respect.

V. The Englishman knows his boys' difficulties. He knows what not to teach: he knows what to begin by teaching and he knows where to lay stress. He looks at the task from the same side as his pupils. The native runs into details and cannot understand certain difficulties.

VI. With English teachers the Form master can take his Form (very often if not always) in their Modern Languages, and this advantage must rank very high for those of us who value most highly the unity of the Form, its social influences, the shepherding which one man can do if he sees the same boys together often; while we recognise also the injustice for the sake of this unity of making Latin and Greek the staple of Form teaching whether best for the members of it or no.

VII. I do not value the power to conduct the lesson in the foreign tongue very highly. The round of remarks which it involves is very limited; Lisez, traduisez, asseyez-vous, continuez, qu'est-ce qu'il a dit, répétez, a-t-il raison, vous avez tort; Aufgepasst, sprechen Sie deutlich, kein dummes Zeug soon degenerate into jargon. While as to the confidence of the Form, unless the English teacher is really incompetent, in which case we need not pity him, I think he will always be sure of quite as much of it as is good for him or necessary for them. I would not, if I could, play pope in my school room, and always speak *ex cathedra*. Wounded vanity often makes a boy question his teacher's judgment no doubt, but you will find that he will back his teacher's opinion against that of all the rest of his companions together if not against his own, and that is I think a moderately fair test. Nor do you lose by admitting your own blunders with due contrition. We all point our teaching often by the blunders in the notes, why not by our own now and then? The boys will at least have a fellow-feeling for you and let you off easily as a lesson to you in the proper treatment of their own cases.

But I do not mean for a moment that I would have no native teacher on my staff. For the few really advanced scholars he is invaluable; he bathes them in the language and opens up its vistas as we cannot hope to do. And you want them as *custodes custodum*, as the teachers of your teachers. I of all men should be ungrateful to forget the ready ample help I have derived from my colleagues in this respect, and there is not one of us who would not say the same. "I do not know, I will ask M. Masson", is my formula.

Nor does what I have said apply to those native teachers whose knowledge of English rivals their knowledge of their own tongue, and whose knowledge of English boys rivals their knowledge of English literature. I should be sorry to teach a set of boys in competition with Professor Buchheim, but I think the Professor would acknowledge that there are not very many like himself. We are not alone in England in thinking this. In Germany English is taught by German teachers, and in France the teaching of English is gradually passing into the hands of Frenchmen, and so in my opinion this important question will be permanently and satisfactorily settled.

LECTURE II.

LECTURE II.

I WISH my second Lecture to be a practical exposition of the actual methods and difficulties of teaching French and German, but I must ask you first to give me a few moments of your patience, while I try to clear up my position in regard to what is rather theory than practice.

I have declared for a system in the main of English teachers for English boys, for plunging into a book, *i.e.* into actual life, as soon as possible, for not thinking too highly of conversation, for Grammar teaching with caution, and, for the linking from the first of synthesis, or use of knowledge, with analysis, or the discovery of it. The teacher must also make up his mind as to the minimum and maximum of time which he will claim for his subject, as to the order in which he will teach the facts, as to the extent to which he will use pure memory.

I. *Time.* The actual minimum in our Public Schools is two hours weekly, and these are naturally assigned to one Modern Language only at a time. Now I say plainly, that is not enough; and, if any of you are asked to undertake to teach Modern Languages on this basis to half a school of four-hundred boys, I counsel you in all earnestness to decline.

I have seen another great subject—Natural Science—discredited by a system which imposed a similar task upon teachers who could have produced good results with fair opportunities. Multiplicity of subjects is a serious danger to Public School education, and we should set our face against ornamental time-tables which seem to promise omniscience. But if to two full schools with preparation can be added an evening's exercise or an hour and a half in school for Composition, then with one language, much good can be done. You will still mainly aim at giving the power to read with ease and to write *tant bien que mal* and be content to prepare your boys to learn to speak rather than dream that you can teach them actually to do so; but this can be done, and this is much. And for keeping up a knowledge of one language far less will suffice—a single school weekly, or a book read out of school, or a weekly prose, so that if boys come to us at fourteen knowing French fairly we may well start the best of them at seventeen or earlier upon German, and in two years give them some facility in reading it. By those who do not learn Greek more time can be given, and both French and German can be commenced from the first. In any case you will try to secure as frequent lessons as possible. Two hours a day for five days in the week, and one or one and a half of preparation is not too much, remembering that for Upper boys your French, if not your German, will largely mean history.

For instance, a time-table of 10 or 12 hours Modern Languages, 8 or 9 Mathematics, 3 or 4 Latin, 1 Literature, 2 Natural Science, 1 Divinity, 2 History, is a reasonable arrangement, where Modern Languages and Mathematics are the staple, though I am by no means an advocate of a rigid time-table, but of free specializing of individual boys.

II. *Order*. In the first place language is not as Euclid, a series of propositions each assuming and depending on the preceding. it is not a skein which can only be unwound from one end. You may attack it from many sides at once, and it consists to a very great extent of isolated words and facts. Much is purely accidental, not logical, and has either no known explanation or only an historical one. Arrangement is therefore only a practical art, not a science, and beyond the obvious principle that the simple must precede the complex, and that you must group and arrange in order to grasp and remember, I do not think there is any rigid principle at all. But as a matter of practice it is so much easier to learn all kindred things in similar ways, that, where languages are taught systematically, it is very important to assimilate nomenclature, order of grouping, and system of analysis in syntax. As, therefore, Latin Grammar is almost universally taught, I would so far as possible call things in French Grammar by the terms used in Latin. Nominative, Accusative and Dative are not perhaps in themselves so good as Subject, Direct Regimen, Indirect Regimen, but I am sure we gain by adopting them. Subject and Object I may say by the way are confusing words to minds both young and old. I heartily agree too with a proposal made lately in the *Journal of Education* to call the tenses by the same name as far as possible in all languages, and though Final and Consecutive are not ideal names, I would certainly adopt them for French Syntax as well as Latin, and in German similarly use the term *Oratio Obliqua* or " Indirect Speech ".

III. *Memory*. There are two typical ways of using the memory which are both in their way necessary.

There lie between them numerous other memorial processes and artifices which are interesting and serviceable. Of the two which stand in contrast I will speak now. The first is the purely mechanical memory acquired by sheer repetition, with I think hardly a trace of reflection in it. We use it for instance for the multiplication table, we add by it, we know our alphabet so (though I am not sure that we need so learn it). Its nature indicates its function; we use it where, if we could, we would use an extraneous machine. Minds differ much in this capacity but all possess it.

The other type is shown in the power we have of quoting from an author whom we have often read but not learnt; of giving an abstract of a book lately read, etc. It depends upon the intelligence brought to bear and the interest excited and upon a special capacity in which minds differ greatly, and which seems in some to be almost absent. We generally call the first parrot memory, though I do not use the term reproachfully. It learns more than it wants, for future mechanical use. The other reproduces such of its impressions as are so vivid as to be always in the mind—it illustrates the law of the survival of the fittest.

How will you use them? Which will you rely on most? If you rely on the first, you will give the child the grammar and make him learn all the verbs, declensions, genders, straight on end, and drive hard until all is known. Your pupil will be well adapted to floor grammar papers, and will be a pest to all his masters by the possession of a hole and corner knowledge which he cannot apply. If you simply rely upon familiarity and recurrence you will find your pupil somewhat abroad without his book, and possessed of a great deal more knowledge than he can state clearly, whereas the other was possessed of much that he could state clearly but could not use. And your second pupil will pass examinations ill, even if examinations are framed as they ought to be (and for the most now are) to test real usable knowledge and not reproduction of lists. Now examinations of some sort, if an evil, are still a necessary evil. You must therefore combine the two. You will give as little as you can to be learnt multiplication-table-wise, and you will find that you can save much by *grouping* your syntax teaching; making your pupil know his way about his books well; making him do plenty of exercises, and every now and then by a sacrifice of intelligence and advance, devoting some lessons to sheer memory practice. Perhaps the minimum of such work in Grammar is a type of each declension, of each conjugation, a few rules, a few jingles, a few very short lists of exceptions and the like. I do not include in this category the main rules of syntax because as I shall state at length, though the memory must be brought to bear upon them, they must not be learnt as so many pages of repetition. And for the sake of saving time from work of this kind for work that is really intellectual, I would keep much in the background in grammar, *e.g.* in beginning German never mention a strong plural feminine for some weeks nor a subjunctive mood for a quarter. If some crop up in your lessons translate them and pass on or hush them up. After a while another step may be taken :—you go back to your strong plurals, exhibit the type to which they conform and add that too to your stock of things that must be absolutely known. In this way the grammar slowly becomes an intelligible possession, the parts of which are known in proportion as they are of frequent occurrence or of importance otherwise. It can, if necessary, be worked up to a specious (I had almost said spurious) degree of accuracy for examination purposes—meanwhile it is commensurate with the pupils' progress.

Shall we admit Memoria Technica? I think not except to a very limited extent. For instance I always teach the inseparable prefixes in German in a rhyme

> Be ge ent emp er *and* ver
> Miss voll hinter wider zer

and we all find the use of a few such forms, but used systematically in my opinion it is a dangerous and undignified method. I know that anything can be got into a rigmarole from the Old Testament History to the genders of Latin substantives, but I believe its efficacy to depend chiefly upon bad examining. There is something degrading to learning in the fact that the scholar must travel through twenty lines of gibberish to run down the gender of one poor word. While he was learning the lines he might have learnt, by the proper method of using the words in composition, and by reading them several times in a book, a good proportion of the list in his rigmarole, and have been spared the danger of believing that salvation for the linguist lies in gender-dodging. We have given up thinking that strings of dates are history, and we should also give up thinking that language consists of lists of irregularities. But if the teacher improvises little harmless modes of exhibiting rules to the eye, if too much is not made of them, I should be almost inclined to say, so long as they are not in print, they may be regarded as allowable devices or relaxations. And the same applies to grotesque and comic examples. We must not be forbidden to speak truth jestingly, but we should not think of giving our pupils the Comic History of England for their text book. However, in the privacy of this

Lecture Room I may be perhaps allowed to give to a few the ephemeral publicity of the black board.

You find stupid boys more stupid than usual over the Past Participle rule perhaps :—write up on your black board,

with *je* SU*is* the Participle agrees with the SU*bject*

with *j'Ai* ,, ,, ,, ,, Accusative

if the accusative has preceded; and you will find it a useful prophylactic against the blunders which have been vexing you.

And this ingenious device, for which I am indebted to a colleague to whom I owe much else, is typical of the proper function of such devices. It is best that a boy should *understand* the reason why the Participle with *être* agrees with the subject, and only use his memory to tell him the less intelligible fact that with *avoir* it agrees with the object only if the object has preceded it, but it is better that your device should make him follow the rule than that his incapacity should continue to let him break it.

Here is another supplied by the same colleague. Your grammar gives you correctly the Relative and Interrogative Pronouns and shews clearly the distinction between Persons and Things. But *que* means so much in French that even intelligent boys go wrong. Shew the pronoun thus

Relative.

	Persons	Things
Nominative	Qui	Qui
Accusative		Que
Genitive		Dont
Dative	à qui	*borrows from* lequel.
		[i.e. borrows a disjunctive form.]

INTERROGATIVE.

	Persons	Things
Nom. and Acc.	QuI	QuE.

Genitive and Dative borrow the Disjunctive form.

de qui   de quoi
à qui   à quoi

A boy never forgets 'Relative Qui Qui for persons and things, IntErrogative QuI QuE' and avoids the most frequent slip of *ce que* for *ce qui*, and *quoi* for *que* in questions, and various other solecisms known only to those who teach the elements of French.

Again in German boys confuse in exercises, and mistranslate in reading *vor* and *seit* used of time. You can settle the matter and teach them *auf*, used of time, also by the following diagram.

Vor is used of a definite point in past time, *seit* carries you from a definite point of past time down to the time of which you speak (these govern the Dative), *auf* takes you from the time of which you speak to a definite point in the future and it governs the Accusative.

You may add as an instance—*Die Abhandlungen waren vor einem Jahre in vollem Gange, aber seit den letzten Monaten sind Hindernisse eingetreten, und daher ist alles aufs folgende Jahr aufgeschoben.*

Mr Phillpotts'[1] has even tried to settle the difficult declensions of German substantives by a set of stories in each of which all the substantives have the same irregularity of declension and in each of which the list is exhaustive. As *tours de force* they are wonderful and one is almost literature. I will read it to you. "The great guilds had commanded, in order to secure their revenues, that the poor bride should spend the whole night on a bench in the horrible cleft—a veritable grave. Here she was to sew with fettered hands a seam of such length, as no two maid-servants of the town could manage. If she could not finish it, she was to be killed with the axe. There she sat in great anguish, as no escape was to be seen, and she beat her breast with her fists till she tore off the skin. Soon she saw passing by a cow, to which she made known her distress, but the cow shewed no desire to help her. The same happened with a goose and a sow which were eating nuts and fruits close by the bride. 'May they turn to sausages,' she exclaimed, 'since they will employ for me neither their strength nor their arts.' The last meeting she had was with a little mouse which had crept forth out of the wall. 'My power is insignificant,' said the mouse, 'but I can gnaw through the strings.' That she really did, and the bride stepped out into the open air."

I have dictated that one to a set of boys and made them learn both English and German; there are some useful prepositions and verbs and phrases in it, so that the process was not merely the acquisition of one particular list of nouns. On the whole I was pleased with the result, but

---

[1] *German Grammar*, Phillpotts and Glünicke. Rivingtons.

it took longer to get the story really known than I had expected, and I doubt the wisdom of trying to use all the stories with the chance of getting them mixed.

So with regard to all memoria technica, comic or serious, I would advise you to feel your way and make your own selection. As teachers you will be glad to know most devices, but you will not discharge your whole bag of tricks.

I will now take the accidence of French and German Grammar in the order in which it is generally presented, and endeavour to distinguish between what we should teach by sheer memory at the outset and what should be left to be merely referred to or perhaps read through and acquired gradually as our pupils advance in the languages.

The first chapter of your French Grammar deals with the alphabet, accents, stops, et cetera. I would teach the alphabet and the three accents, explaining that accent does not mean *stress* but only a difference of sound, but *not* saying anything about their history; I would teach the *cedilla*, the *tréma* and no more, and I would only expect a boy to say 'that is *accent aigu*,' 'that vowel has the *tréma*,' etc., and not to say 'There are three accents in French, etc. etc.' I would leave stops alone for the present; when a boy does dictation he at once learns them. There are other facts in this chapter such as elisions, the *trait d'union*, capital letters, etc. These also I would leave alone. A clever boy will probably read the rest of the chapter for himself and remember a good deal of it, and I think this is wholly good. To leave an unknown something at every turn, which you say will be intelligible and useful when he knows more, stimulates him to rise to the higher level of which he hears, and leads him to learn for himself and by himself and to ask questions—a quite inestimable advantage. Some Grammars distinguish the necessary portion from this fuller exposition by printing the latter in small print; a useful device open only to the objection that from fear of the critics too much is generally classed as necessary. Some again print the two portions on opposite pages, and this is even better in my opinion, though liable to the same danger.

Next come the Articles, which of course we teach from the first, and you will find *l'* = both *le* and *la*, and the forms *au, aux* need special emphasis. The only point of controversy is, Shall we recognise the so-called Partitive Article or not? I say 'Yes' with some confidence. It is logically if not historically an Article; but the paramount reason for so classing it and teaching it from the first, is that it makes the Syntax of the Article very much easier when your pupil gets so far. And the Syntax of the Article is indisputably hard. If under the head of Partitive Article your Grammar gives you besides the history of it so much the better. If your pupil has an opinion of his own as to whether *du* is an article or not he is in a fair way to become a scholar, and the teacher always has it in his power to prevent him from also becoming a prig.

When a child reaches the next section which deals with the Nouns Substantive and Adjective he very commonly and justifiably conceives a disgust for a language so full of foolish rules, and of exceptions with whose perversity he would sympathize if he did not have to learn them. Well, say boldly 'I will not compel my pupil to learn them at all.' Tell him that the French plural is formed by adding *s*, but that *-au, -eu, -ou*, add *x* not *s*, and that *-al* becomes *-aux* as in the article, and that *-s, -x, -z* do not change.

Then, since the words are of very frequent occurrence, you may require the following list to be learnt:

> bal makes bals,
> travail ,, travaux,
> bijou ,, bijoux,
> genou ,, genoux,
> ciel ,, cieux,
> œil ,, yeux,

making your pupil say an instance of each, e.g. *Les yeux bleus vont aux cieux* which contains three exceptional words *yeux, bleus, cieux*; but observe that you must have the sentence written by your pupil, or you cannot be sure that he is sound.

Why should you teach more? There are other exceptions you will say in the grammar, and as you come across the words you will note them. What is the worst that can happen? The child writes *caillous* and you correct it and in time it learns the right plural. As to adjectives, you will simply say they make their plurals like nouns but *bleu* makes *bleus*.

Feminines, you will say, add *e*, and

> -er makes -ère,
> -f ,, -ve,
> -eux ,, -euse,

and there are other very special rules, so that whenever you come across an adjective you should say the feminine just as you should always say the article with a noun for the sake of marking the gender. But do not use the lists in your grammar for repetition lessons: use them for reference.

For genders of nouns you give as rules to be learnt by heart that -*ie*, -*ion*, -*çon*, -*son* are feminine and that other consonant endings are mostly masculine. If you try to do more you have a term's work before you, and confusion at the end. Let the gender be learned with the words by means of the article, trust to time and tell your pupil to refer to his lists. There exists a card for French Genders drawn up in dictionary shape which is not a bad companion for writing exercises, but we must not multiply books, and a good grammar and dictionary should be all that we allow.

Plurals of Compound Nouns.

This section is an instrument of torture which should be relegated to the Museum together with the rack, the thumb-screws and the boot, and a record inserted in Haydn's Dictionary of the date when it was last used.

You must have nothing learnt here; but you may point out that common sense settles most of the cases already, and that it will probably in time settle all. The Academy now allows the form *autodafés*.

Comparison of Adjectives.

The accidence is simple, though the syntax is not altogether so. But you must spend some time in insisting upon the difference between *meilleur* and *mieux*

pire ,, *pis*,
moindre ,, *moins*,

for confusion is easy and the words are of very frequent occurrence.

Pronouns.

If you have begun by teaching a simple verb by having its tenses said in little sentences, as I suggested in my last lecture, and have followed up this by other easy sentences and some written exercises, the pronouns will have learnt themselves by dint of frequent recurrence. You are now however in teaching grammar teaching your pupil to analyse and to recognise the different cases and persons by name. You will therefore be right in making him say the personal pronouns separately Sing. *Je, me, me,* Plur. *nous, nous, nous,* etc. and you will find that the 3rd person needs some care with its confusing *lui.* By all means also classify these into conjunctive and disjunctive: the names are well chosen and the distinction real and practical. Let the reflexive pronouns be said thus: *Je me, tu te,* $\genfrac{}{}{0pt}{}{il}{elle}$ *se, nous nous, vous vous,* $\genfrac{}{}{0pt}{}{ils}{elles}$ *se,* and point out that *soi* is the disjunctive form of *se.*

You will find no trouble with the possessive pronouns: *son* for *sa* before a vowel and *h* mute and *leur* not *leure* for the feminine are the only difficulties.

The predicate forms *le mien,* etc. must of course be learnt and one would expect that they would be wrongly used; but as a matter of experience, while reflexives and personal pronouns are perplexing, I do not find that the possessives are so, and such mistakes as *les nos* for *les nôtres* are very rare.

The demonstrative *ce,* invariable, should be passed over in my opinion in learning accidence. When you come to the syntax of the pronouns you may call attention to it, taking care that it has previously been used freely in the sentences which you have learnt.

So again if you will use a table of variations, such as that given on p. 19, you will teach *celui* easily and you need not trouble about rules for it.

I would deal with the relatives also synthetically, i.e. by sentences and tables of variations at first. I have already given an ingenious device for saving the confusion which naturally arises from the great similarity of forms. As to *lequel* and its uses as relative and interrogative the difficulties belong not to accidence but to syntax. The declension is simple.

Regular Verbs.

I need not stop long over the regular verbs. *Être* and *avoir* are known, we assume, from the first. The four types of conjugation must be learnt also. Some grammars give two types for the second, *finir* and *dormir*. I cannot agree with this: I am quite sure that it is better to class the few verbs which follow *dormir* as irregular.

So soon as the four types are learnt, teach also the formation of tenses. It should be given in all grammars in a way that is clear to the eye.

(1) From the present participle are formed the plurals of the present indicative and the present subjunctive and the imperfect indicative (with a special note on the 3rd conjugation where this requires a slight modification for the 3rd plural pres. ind. and the sing. and 3rd plural of the subjunctive).

(2) From the infinitive are formed the future and conditional.

(3) From the 2nd pers. sing. of the preterite is formed the imperfect subjunctive.

Any deviation from these rules or from the four types of the conjugations should be treated as irregular.

Irregular Verbs.

Have a list with full statement of them.

Shall you group it by the conjugations? No, I think not. You want it above all things to be easy of reference; and though this plan may be more scientific, the alphabetical is far more serviceable. But because it is to be for reference, see that the verb is stated at *full* length, as clearly to the eye as can be. Now do not set this list to be learned, but as each irregular verb occurs, refer to the list and have that one learned—or rather do not have a verb learned until you have come across it three times in your construing. In this way, you will learn first what comes oftenest, and remember that by a special providence irregular verbs occur very frequently. When—which will not be soon—you have come across nearly all your list, the boy may learn them, and irregular verbs may form a repetition lesson (or lessons) to be kept up each term.

But of all irregular verbs, the French are the worst— they are irregular in such outrageous ways; how are they to be remembered but by sheer repetition? If, however, you will adopt the plan that I have given you, you will get them known long before the pupil has his other knowledge on the same level and you will get them learned without tears. Do you remember Heine's sentence about irregular verbs? "The irregular verbs," he says, "are distinguished from the regular verbs in that they entail more floggings." If we cannot alter that state of things we had better not teach them at all.

Adverbs.

Leave them at first to take care of themselves. Very soon the observation that '*ment*' is the regular adverb formation obtrudes itself. There is also the curious change *-amment -emment* from *-ant -ent*. So soon as this has been noticed by your pupil, or a good opportunity occurs for calling his attention to it, you may tell him—because it is interesting, and good training—the origin of the French adverb. It is admirably done, as indeed is all work of this kind, in Brachet's *Public School French Grammar*, a book which no teacher has ever taken an advanced pupil through at a rapid rate without being sensible of the flood of light that it throws upon dark corners, of the new aids to memory which it gives, and of the real introduction which it is to French etymology. But I reserve my remarks upon this point—only saying that the reason why the feminine adjective is used to form the adverb once grasped, further small rules for its formation are very soon correctly got by heart.

Conjunctions.

If you will use Prendergast's list of variations, either with his own sentences or better still with those of your making, you will as a matter of fact get the conjunctions known. And here as in all cases, if they are known in two ways, you are very wrong to wish them to be known in a third. If the boy knows the English when he sees them, and if he knows the French for them when he sees the English, which the variation will enable him to do, why in the name of common sense should you want him also to rattle off the conjunctions in an alphabetical and comparatively useless list? That is the sort of learning that was once so rife, and so detrimental to all progress. It is possible that he may not think more about the one than about the other, but the first two processes are the only processes used in translating and composing:

the other can only be useful for the one man in a million who may have to teach grammar out of his head without a book, or for the examinations in grammar, framed for those who have learned grammar in this way, which are happily becoming almost extinct. I have nothing more to say about French accidence, but if it is dealt with in this way the child (for it is chiefly children who will deal with French accidence, inasmuch as this will be almost always the earliest foreign language taught) will not have been confused; he will have been made to observe, and to learn by observing and by familiarity, and by making his own lists, and will not have found the process dull. When you have gone through the accidence in this way, you may keep it up as you please. Probably then you will simply have it learned from the book; but even then I hope that the lists of exceptions will not be overmuch insisted upon.

German accidence.

Inasmuch as there are three genders, as many declensions as you like to make, each with an attendant train of exceptions—if you like to make them—there is no doubt that the beginnings of German accidence are more formidable than the beginnings of French. The battle of the declensions is not yet over. New systems for arranging them appear I really believe at the rate of one a week—the reason for this being that when each teacher has mastered them, dropped into his own system, and has found, as we all find, that we can teach them upon any system, he is brought to think that his system is the best. Certainly, I am no exception to this rule. I am quite convinced that mine is the best. The only reason I can give you for agreeing with me, is certainly not that I can teach by that method better than any other; but that I have found some people, whose opinion you and I would respect, to agree with me :—that it has been worked for some years, and that we have seen no reason to change it. The battle of course centres round this point. Will you try so to group your varieties as to make your lists of exceptions few, or will you try to make as few declensions as possible, and relegate all the exceptions to lists which are not more numerous than those of the other system, but certainly each contain more words? If you belong to the first side, you will have at least five declensions : if you belong to the second, you will recognise only two, the strong and the weak ; and indeed you will recognise only one—the strong. Though I am quite aware that philology is not sure that the weak is not the older of the two, still the strong is obviously the real declension ; the weak may be treated as a mere termination. Indeed I do not think that from the very first it is a bad thing to reason about it, and to say that the termination '*en*' is simply put on as a sign that the word is to be declined somehow—as a mark that it is not in the nominative case. And it is used in the same way in the adjectives, whenever you have already marked the case by a strong termination preceding ; and it is probably the origin of that curious use of the infinitive in place of the past participle, in compound tenses. The root plus '*en*' is an apology for, is the ghost of an inflection. That may or may not be true, but at least it has the merit, which is all that many scientific hypotheses can boast of, that it is a very good thread to string your facts on ; and that it more or less strikes the imagination. I know no book more interesting in this way than Mr Keane's *True Theory of German Declension and Conjugation.*

I believe then in teaching, as the one German declension, the strong type. You will exhibit this to the eye. For some time I used to like to have the terminations only given as the type, until I was wholly convinced, by others' evidence as well as my own, that it was better to take a word. Let us take Hut: Singular Hut, Hut, Hutes, Hute—that is all; Plural Hüte, Hüte, Hüte, Hüten—that is all. The only change in the plural is the umlaut and the dative. All datives end in *en*, but they don't add an extra one if the word already ends with it—that is the strong declension. Some words are weak—they add *en* to all cases singular and plural. Feminine words are undeclined in the singular. Their plurals are weak. Then follow simple rules, soon learned, as to which words are strong and which weak; and then sundry lists. These lists take the place of the multitudinous declensions of other grammars. The difficulty, and you do not blink the difficulty, lies in the German plural. Monosyllables, you teach, if masculine modify the root vowel in the Plural, other words do not. List I. contains the few words that are weak because they are, not because they come under your already given rule. List II. the feminines which, in spite of the rule you have given, make a strong plural. List III. the words that add *er* in the plural, and these you point out *all* modify. List IV. (a long one)—the words that do not modify in the plural, being otherwise regular. List V. dissyllables which do modify, in spite of your rule. Lists VI. and VII. the mixed declension, i.e. the words of which the first group make *-ens* in the genitive, and the rest weak, while the latter with a strong singular have a weak plural. The separate declension usually given for words in *-el -en -er*, is simply a rule of euphony and you teach it as such: the *e* of the inflection is dropped because it is easier to pronounce the word without it. Now of course, if you try to learn these lists, the task would be harder than an elaborate system of declensions, but you need not and ought not. You learn the first, that is the general rules and the type of the strong declension, and the lists you treat as a dictionary to be referred to, to lie open whilst all exercises are being done, to be learned very gradually and never to be said by heart at all. I have already given you the ingenious plan by which these lists have been made easy to remember (if you must remember them) by placing the words of each in a specially written story, and I have told you why upon the whole I do not think that it is quite worth the doing. But I do not feel sure that my opinion will not change, and I should like to know the experience of actual teachers. The book has not been out long, and I have given you all the means of testing it for yourselves.

Genders.

By all means give your pupils if they are not in their grammars, and if they are there make them learn, the following rules, the exceptions are so few.

Masc. terminations : *-el, -en, -er, -ling.*
Fem.   „   *-e, -ei, -heit, -keit, -schaft, -ung, -in, -inn.*
Neuter   „   *-sal, -sel, -thum.*

Neuter are also words with prefix 'ge', infinitives used as substantives, and diminutives, that is the terminations *-chen* and *-lein*. If that is known, or even before it is known—if it is open to the eye, you need not concern yourselves very seriously about the genders to begin with. As in French, in speaking of words always say them with the article prefixed, and then the gender is gradually acquired; and in writing exercises where the discovery of the gender is often a serious trouble, involving reference to the dictionary, try if a plan which I always adopt is not a good expedient. The words which follow these rules the pupils are expected to know; those that break them are very numerous, but they are also very common words—the feature of exceptions in general. I indicate these by placing one dot under them for masculines, two for feminines, and three for neuter. I am supposing that you use exercises (as I think undoubtedly you ought for beginners) which supply all the German words, only leaving the pupil to inflect them and place them in order. The only book of any length that I know which does this is Mullins' Exercises[1], and I wish that that book were longer. I must also say that I wish the English were a little more attractive. But if you have in your room a large blackboard, and all school-rooms should have one, you will find that it does not take long to write on it every word that your pupils want for doing their German Prose, and then you can indicate the gender in the way I have suggested.

Adjective rule.

If declension and gender are hard, adjectives are hardly less so—there is no doubt about that. I have mentioned Mr Keane's interesting theory, but one must say plainly that the theory will not do to teach as the elementary instruction in the German adjective. The teachers with whom I work have a concordat on adjective rule. We all used to teach

---

[1] *Easy German Exercises.* D. Nutt.

it differently, but at last we compromised the matter. The result has been satisfactory, and here is the rule if you care to have it.

1. Adjectives used as Predicates are undeclined.
2. ,, ,, ,, Attributes without Article are declined strong, i.e. like *der* etc.
3. ,, ,, ,, Attributes with Article end in -*en*, except the Five (i.e. the Nominatives and Fem. and Neut. Acc. of the Singular). These five after *der* etc. end in *e*, after *ein* etc. are strong.

You explain that *der* etc., means *dieser*, *jener*, and all the words which are so declined, and *ein* etc. means *ein*, *kein* and the Possessive Pronouns. This rule, which you will admit is soon learnt, has now to become instinctive. You will find boys learn it at various paces, and you will find them forget it in exactly the inverse ratio to the pace at which they have learned it. But you can soon get it picked up again, and you ought never to start in any term upon exercises, until it is fairly well known. One page of sentences framed to show it in all its glory with the undeclined German words opposite, will serve you as practice ground for all time. So soon as your pupil makes a mistake, send him back. If he is an older pupil send him into the furthest corner of the room to do elementary adjective sentences in disgrace, until he knows better. You may get some fun out of it by bantering your boys on their slips, and if you like by pitting them one against the other and having a Form match. I must however say that personally I do not like the latter way of getting a stimulus. While you are teaching this you will also have made them familiar with the cases of the article, and of the nouns themselves, and that is a considerable advantage in a language that has so many terminations still extant, as the German. Has it ever occurred to you, to digress for a moment, what a blessing the Norman Conquest proved to our mother tongue? You may or you may not think an inflectional language a more beautiful instrument of speech than an analytical one like the English of the present day, but you must admit that one which is almost wholly analytical is much better than one that gives you all the trouble of learning terminations, and yet treats speech mainly analytically, as the German does. Now at the time of the Norman Conquest the English tongue went underground so to speak for some two hundred years—and became literally the vernacular.

It was not spoken in any courts of Law, nor in Church, nor by anyone of gentle birth. It was spoken chiefly by the serfs, and it was hardly written at all. As a result it dropped its terminations with very great rapidity. When it emerged again into literature with the revivified feeling of nationality at the beginning of the Hundred Years War it had lost the greater part of its terminations, and it has now nearly lost them all. If only we had adopted or could adopt a system of phonetic spelling, the English Language would be the easiest to learn in the whole world. It is destined probably—if any language is—to be the universal language of mankind, and though this is not the subject of my lecture, I cannot forbear to say that it is for you who belong to the younger generation to consider whether you will not make the sacrifice—a great one I admit—involved in the adoption of a phonetic system, for the sake of adding at least one whole year of intellectual work to the school time of all the children in all the Board Schools in England, or if you decide that that year is not wanted, for the sake of letting them start in their career of bread-winning one year earlier. But that is by the way. Meantime there is German with all its inflections waiting to be learned.

Prepositions.

Prepositions cannot but be as troublesome as genders. You have not only three cases that they may govern, but some of them govern two each, and some are placed after their case. I recommend a clearly printed list in your grammar and that this list be referred to, and the prepositions learnt gradually by exercises and above all by the proverbs and examples which you will have committed to memory. But this is not all. There is the syntax of the prepositions, and you may treat this from the German side, or you may group the prepositions by their English use, which has its advantages for composition. A complete grammar must certainly contain a syntax from the German side, that your pupil may know where to find his information; but the other arrangement is so useful, that you will probably use both plans. They are extremely well done in at least half a dozen grammars. You clearly do not want boys to learn all this by heart, but it is pleasant reading for your elder boys. They see at once how useful it is; it lends itself to questions; and the examples, if well chosen, will illustrate much else besides the use of the prepositions, and form a substantial part of your teaching. If you have a boy with a quick memory, and a turn for poetry, you may show him two stanzas of four lines each in which some ingenious German has grouped all the commoner prepositions—

PHILEMON AN SEINEN FREUND.

Durch dich ist die Welt mir schön, *ohne dich* würde ich sie hassen;
Für dich lebe ich ganz allein, *um dich* will ich gern erblassen;
Gegen dich soll kein Verleumder ungestraft sich je vergeh'n,
Wider dich kein Feind sich waffnen; ich will dir zur Seite steh'n.

DAPHNIS AN DIE QUELLE.

Nach dir schmachte ich, *zu dir* eile ich, du geliebte Quelle du!
Aus dir schöpfe ich, *bei dir* ruhe ich, sehe dem Spiel der Wellen zu.
Mit dir scherze ich, *von dir* lerne ich heiter durch das Leben wallen,
Angelacht *von Frühlingsblumen* und begrüsst *von Nachtigallen*.

Irregular Verbs.

The strong verbs are now quite rightly not called irregular, but they must be placed in alphabetical order in the grammar, and, as in French, you will find that alphabetical order is better than the grouping by similar sound-changes. And you will not find them a serious difficulty. The verbs themselves come extremely often in ordinary speech and writing: they learn themselves if you give three minutes in your construing lesson to running through the principal parts of them. The really irregular verbs in German are few, and they also are common.

The passive verb in German must take a little longer than in French because of its peculiar use of *werden*. Tell an intelligent boy that where we use 'to be' the German says 'to become', and that he must say *worden* not *geworden*; and he will work them out correctly. But you will probably find it best to have the tenses said rather often in the form of easy sentences so that they may become familiar. Similarly with the subjunctive, point out to a clever boy the difference between one present subjunctive and its present indicative, and for him the subject is practically at an end, except indeed for the verbs, which will be in his list, which modify. And the past subjunctive is easier still; you simply tell him that the strong verb modifies if it can, and that others do not. As in French, the short form of the Compound Conditional must be dwelt upon and taught by instances. Just because it is short you will find boys pick it up readily. There remains the formation of words in German both by suffix and prefix. This will form a chapter in your grammar, that will be set to be read, then questioned on. If well treated, it is extremely interesting, and every teacher will have a pet selection of instances, especially of such very idiomatic prefixes as *er- ver- ent-*.

Syntax.

Before running through the chief points in the syntax of the two languages, it is worth while to say that here you will only use the second kind of memory and not the first— that is to say, you will have the rules read and expounded and attended to, the examples translated and dissected, small exercises set on them, and all this enforced by each construing lesson. By this backward and forward process, this analysis and synthesis, you will gradually work up to the fullest amount of knowledge that the time and the pupils' brains will admit of. Above all things remember that the rule is only useful as a clear statement—as a clear grouping of facts; that the instance is more valuable than the rule, and that the power to apply the instance to make fresh examples is the test of real and fruitful knowledge. That process if any may be fitly called the 'training faculty'. Never be a slave to your rules, and you must take great care that your pupils do not become slaves.'

Do you know the story of Jean Paul Richter's quarrel with his teacher? "Why is that so?" said the teacher. No answer. "You have a splendid memory and I know you can tell me—why don't you do so?" No answer. And as Heine says, *Es regnete Prügel*.

When the storm was over and the head boy had been in disgrace for the whole day, he confessed why he had not answered. " He wanted me to say 'because the rule is so and so', and it is not because the rule says so, it is so because it is, and the rule only states the fact." Now remember that the boy was right, wholly right, and if for shortness' sake you may say "because the rule says so", do not forget that it is only for shortness' sake. Every now and then you must make your pupils talk rationally about the rules. I have been so much impressed by the necessity of this as a part of the intellectual training, that I have long had drawn up a set of grammar questions of an easy kind which lead up to the well-known rules in a slightly different way, and which I expect my boys to be able to talk about reasonably. I make them pass an examination in this kind of syntax once a term, and there is no doubt that this important part of the language, when you really are beginning to use it as a conscious instrument of speech, needs the teacher's personal and so far as possible individual attention more than any other. Boys, even clever boys, will not learn for themselves. True, you may set them the exercises on the syntax in a good exercise book based on a good grammar, but you must well talk about them first and you must go over this process again and again. All teachers know how at the beginning of each term they feel as if their boys had forgotten all they ever knew. If your teaching is systematized and your divisions are well graded one into the other, you will have an agreement as to the amount which is expected to be known in each division—the minimum I mean, not the maximum, though you will find that the minimum is the maximum. These syntax schools, or prose schools as they are called, are based by most of us upon the plan long adopted in teaching the classics, and in my opinion quite rightly. Have your boys in during the whole time; do not set them anything to prepare. Thus you have an hour and a half or two hours for continuous work. A piece of prose or a long exercise is the main work, but you want every moment of your time as teacher to be employed to the very best advantage. I suggest to you the following plan as being found in practice to be a great deal the most useful. Begin, the boys having their books open probably before them, though this is not essential, by calling their attention to the points which you are going to teach them as a fresh lesson or to take them over again. Illustrate orally as well as you can—then probably you will give them two or three minutes to look at the book now explained and at the examples. Then set them not less than three nor more than six well chosen sentences, and make your own. You will be surprised and pleased to find how good you become at inserting into the example which just hits off the new knowledge, one or two points that involve last week's or last fortnight's or last month's or last term's teaching; and so you keep your knowledge together. Most of us who have taught for any time have a large selection of MS. sentences of this kind which we are always adding to and improving. Let these sentences be done with all books closed. Give orally what help you judge fit;—in this way you will avoid what is a serious danger, that of having your class fairly capable of working a thing out with dictionary and grammar, but very unready when they do not possess these helps. Then collect these sentences, and while the boys are doing the bulk of their work call them up individually and look them over. Here again you will find your pace as an overlooker increases very much with practice. Any of you who happen to have done corrections for the press well know how the eye and the hand become, the one accurate, the other quick, and you will be surprised to find how much looking over, correcting, and recorrecting you can get done in the hour and a half. Of course make *the pupil* correct as much as you can, but remember above all things that he must not feel helpless. Have them written out again once at the very least. If you have time the best form of fair copy is to have the whole thing done again. This is true of all written work whatsoever, and the only limitations, though they are serious ones, are those of time and of your boys' patience, for it must be owned that the process may soon become wearisome.

In French Syntax you will certainly begin with the article. Almost all grammars, and there are many good ones, group this section in much the same way. There is a good deal of logical training in it, and in French it is undoubtedly hard. Next to the article, perhaps even before it, you may place in French the personal pronouns (*conjunctive and disjunctive*) and their relative positions, and here as a matter of practice you will find that you will be driven to give a rule that must be learnt by heart. The following, adopted by many grammars, is much the shortest and most usable form:

All governed Pronouns precede the verb.
Me, te, se, nous, vous precede all others,
Le, la, les precede *lui, leur, y, en,*
Lui, leur precede *y, en,*
y precedes *en.*

You will observe that if the first two lines are known the rest cannot be forgotten.

Then you have to deal with the Pronouns after Imperatives. Here are four more lines which settle them:

All Pronouns follow the Imperative Affirmative.
Use *moi, toi,* in place of *me, te.*
Accusative precedes Dative, but
y precedes *moi, toi, le, la.*

Va-t-en, Donnez m'en, Frappez-moi mais m'écoutez, serve to illustrate the exceptions to these rules and you teach them as an appendix.

The Syntax of the Adjective is difficult in French because of the intricacy of the rules for its position and the numerous anomalies such as the gender of *gens,* the agreement of *nu, demi* and others. You will be wise to leave the full acquisition of the whole of this section until a very late stage, giving at most the rule that adjectives expressing taste, colour, form, follow the noun; and a select number of sentences illustrating the use of *demi, nu, grand, neuf, sage, dernier,* a number which you may continually enlarge. But do not set the long lists, which are very properly given in your grammar, to be learnt by heart. A sentence is alive, a list is a dead thing. I believe that sentences alone will serve our purpose, but there is no objection to a set of exercises done first with grammar open and then with grammar closed.

The Relative Pronouns must be done by exercises and

sentences thoroughly well worked. The distinction between conjunctives and disjunctives should be worked here as well as with personal pronouns. Then in order of importance come the past participles. You will first explain the common sense of the rule, for it is largely a common sense one, and then give a short statement to aid the memory; for although it is right to appeal to the reason, it must be remembered that in speech you do not reason out everything that you say, nor will you go too deep at first into this: you will leave the difficult cases with infinitive moods to be learnt much later. The subjunctive in French is distinctly difficult. I do not think that an exposition such as alone would satisfy a scholar is feasible for teaching boys. Perhaps Professor Jowett's suggestion that the finer sense of idiom may take the place of rules is true here if anywhere. I am inclined to think that instances are the best way of teaching the elements of it, and a careful analysis of the subjunctives in your construing lessons the best way of teaching it fully. One or two things you will of course work hard, such as the subjunctive with the superlative. There remain the redundant *ne* and the infinitive mood; its absolute use, its use with prepositions, the use of the active infinitive where we use the passive, and lastly what is of such common occurrence in French and really so very hard to grasp—the use of *faire* with the infinitive. Discussing the other day with a colleague the conditions of teaching French syntax, I came to the conclusion that to get this known thoroughly was perhaps the most difficult task of all. As it comes so often, my own opinion is in favour of stating it very fully, and of making the pupil grasp the principle of it, namely that the subject of the infinitive dependent on *faire*, what would be the nominative to the sentence if *faire* were removed and the infinitive turned into the indicative mood, becomes the dative instead of the accusative if the infinitive is transitive —the reason being probably to avoid the collision of two accusatives, e.g.,

> Je le ferai venir, 'I will send for him'.
> Je le lui ferai envoyer, 'I will make him send it'.

You must also point out that the latter may also mean, 'I will have it sent to him', and that in fact the construction, common as it is in French, is an ambiguous and faulty one.

The use of it in writing French is not so important as the need of avoiding the errors arising from it in translating. The following form of it in a long sentence is particularly misleading—

> Je lui ferai dire ce qu'il a fait,

and it is only by pointing out that *il me dira ce qu'il a fait* is the equivalent of it that a boy sees that the analysis of it is the same as that of the simpler case with which he is more familiar.

Then there are the innumerable constructions of *que*. As it represents at least nine Latin words they may well be innumerable. A page or so devoted to it in your grammar, and some time spent in illustrating the instances there and in your construing lessons, is all that you can hope to do for them. You will find the inversion of verb and nominative after the relative *que* especially troublesome to all careless pupils.

As to exercises, you want one book of them set upon your grammar. This will be used out of school. There are many good ones, and more are always appearing, but as, in common with many teachers, I think that the grammar of Eve and de

Baudiss is considerably the best, I am glad that at last there is a full set of exercises as a companion to it. But if all exercise books call attention to the rules on which they are chiefly set, you may adopt any one of them as supplementary books for *viva voce* or for rapid work in school, or for special fragments of classes, keeping the main book for your weekly or bi-weekly exercises.

A few words as to the correction of exercises. I will tell you how you may really lighten this distasteful labour. If you are examining, arrange your papers roughly so that you will look over the best first. Why? Because you will then get to know the full capabilities of the paper. You will mark better, and in examining the mark is the first and almost the only object, and you will look over the best work when your mind is freshest. As you get tired it will be a real relief to come to papers that can be run through with very much greater rapidity. I have found the gain of doing this very great. But in looking over your weekly exercises do exactly the contrary.—Why? Because now you want to correct and to teach, and to find at once all the mistakes for which your eye must be on the look-out. Therefore take the worst boy first. You will have to give him a great deal of time and to re-write a good deal for him, but by the time you have done two of the worst you really know all about the piece; also, you have probably done nearly half your writing. The rest will get better and better till your best boys will need no corrections, but only a few red marks and lines; for you will lay it down as a rule that you will never put more than a mark where that is enough to indicate the necessary correction. By all means have a code of symbols for your corrections. Here is one which my colleagues and I have used for some time—it works very well though I can conceive a better. This at least has the merit of not being very elaborate.

- —— mistake.
- ‑ ‑ bad mistake.
- ⁓⁓ wrong order.
- ∧ omission.
- | wrong accent.
- ↓ place the word at the end of the clause.
- …… find a better word.

Can you have exercises looked over vicariously? I fear the answer must be 'no'. You want to know what points you must insist on because your boys are weak on them. You cannot get this knowledge from looking rapidly over exercises upon which others have done the real work. Again, your exercises give you a series of questions which you fire off in the next few days at the right persons. Always have fair copies done, or at any rate adopt some plan which will make your boys attend to the corrections which you have made. I remember the indignation with which a colleague once told another, who was noted for the elaborate care with which he corrected the VIth Form Latin verses, how he had seen one of the leading boys of the school drop the carefully red-inked exercise in the mud as soon as he was outside the master's door. It was very bad—but it was human nature, and it is with human nature that we have to deal. For reasons of the same kind do not have exercises looked over by the boys themselves. If you have got your boys together in class there are twenty things that you can do with them which are better. You must do the work out of school yourselves. It is sad drudgery, but you will be repaid, and you will be surprised to find how rapidly in time you will come to do it.

In German Syntax you will again begin with the article, but by calling attention to its likeness to English or to French, you will find that your task is here comparatively light. As German is always the second language learnt, if not the third, you will find throughout that the knowledge of one language is of great help to the acquisition of a second or third. Next to the article will come the order of words. Most grammars, with German thoroughness, give a rather elaborate table. My own belief is that the three following rules are all that need be learnt, and they are at least short.

(1) If the nominative does not begin the sentence, the nominative and verb are inverted, except after *und, aber, denn, sondern, allein*.

(2) With a compound tense place the auxiliary as in English and the rest of the verb at the end of the clause in the reverse of the English order.

(3) In all dependent sentences place the whole verb at the end in the reverse of the English order.

If you add to this that the dative precedes the accusative except with personal pronouns, and a statement of what may be called the elegant order where three or more verbs come together at the end of a sentence, which may come much later in your teaching, you may leave the rest, and the rest is really not much, to be acquired by observation and the ear.

Indeed you will have done a good deal before you teach these rules. You will have accustomed your pupils to put simple sentences in their German order, and let them be half conscious of what is right before you give them the explicit statement. One teacher taking a low division always has his German construed in German order, and now and then gives a piece of newspaper to be put into this German order, and not into German words. That is not a bad plan. Most grammars again give special rules as to the position of the separable prefix. You will find if you look into the matter carefully, that these are really covered by my three rules given above. You must of course make your boys familiar with them by a good deal of practice in easy sentences. It is a real exercise of the mind in logic which German children have to be taught as much as English.

Then you will come to the Relatives. These are fairly easy with the exception of *wer* and of the Genitives *dessen, deren, dessen*, where the English tendency is to insert the article afterwards, and to say for instance, 'Ein Zimmer dessen *die* Wände' etc. I always go very fully into the syntax of *wer*, but I find that it takes a long while to eradicate such blunders as 'Der alte Mann, *wer* indessen sich umgesehen hatte'. Indeed my experience is that even boys who have been in Germany, and talk German, make a good many slips of the kind. The Syntax of German adjectives is comparatively easy. You must have your lists of those which demand special prepositions, but you must not teach these by memory. You will probably insist at some length on some few, such as *viel, halb* and perhaps *all*.

You will pass on next to the verbs of mood, to the delicate subtlety of which Professor Earle has rendered a due tribute of admiration in his interesting 'Philology of the English Tongue'. As he rightly says, if these modal verbs had the good fortune to belong to a dead language scholars would be loud in praise of their dainty differences. And if this is true of English, where half the power of them has been lost by our unfortunate use of 'might', 'could', and 'would' as present tenses, it is much more true of German, where the study of them seems to lead into the very arcana of speech. Also, as in French, the difference between 'I ought to have done it' and its kindred forms is most important and can hardly be too much insisted upon. These must be worked until they are instinctive. Here again you will find your Prendergastian table of variations useful.

Then come Infinitives—their use as substantives; their use with and without *zu*; their use where the English uses the verbal 'ing'; the curious substitution already mentioned of an infinitive for a past participle in such a sentence as 'ich hätte es thun wollen', and, following the infinitives, the use of the participles.

The German Subjunctive can be clearly classified as *Potential Optative Conditional* and the Subjunctive of *Indirect Speech*. The latter use will already have been a good deal talked about in construing. Now you will explain it fully and work it by exercises.

I think you will agree that in the points which I have thus briefly run through there is ample ground for some years of training, and that much that I have said must be and can be taught only to fairly advanced pupils. This is quite true, but it is because this teaching is so useful and so necessary that I have said that you cannot teach French and German successfully without more time than is usually given to them.

Some books which are extremely good take the form of a course, 1st, 2nd, 3rd, 4th, 5th, 6th Term, and so on. I cannot think that this is a good plan (though no doubt it is good for the private tuition of individual boys). Your boys advance at such very different rates that you cannot work such a book successfully with a Form or Division; nor is such a book good for reference however full its index; nor again can this method avoid a good deal of repetition.

But I do think that as soon as you begin to teach French and German Prose seriously you want not only a full Accidence and Syntax with an ample index, too often lacking in otherwise good grammars, but also a book dealing with most of the constructions from the English side. This need not be separate from the Prose Book itself, but might well form an introduction to it on the model of Mr Sidgwick's Greek Prose Composition. Such a book is much needed, and none of the existing attempts satisfy me, though many are excellent for certain portions of the Syntax. Messrs Cassal and Karcher's 'French Prose Composition' comes nearest to what I desiderate as regards completeness. But it assumes the form of a dictionary, and I prefer the form of a continuous treatise, though the dictionary has this advantage that it is its own index. As an elementary book Mr Storr's 'Hints on French Syntax' with its excellent series of examples is the best I know.

I will now take as illustrations of how such a system as I have been describing actually works in practice, first a piece of German Prose and then a page of French Construing.

1. I was shown the room destined for me.

2. You deserve to have a statue erected in your honour.

3. You will dine with us to-day, won't you?

In the Rue Blanche there is a butcher who sells dogs, cats, and

1. Dann zeigte man mir das für mich bestimmte Zimmer.

2. Sie verdienen, dass man Ihnen zu Ehre eine Bildsäule errichte.

3. Sie werden heute bei uns zu Mittag essen? nicht wahr?

In der Rue Blanche giebt es einen Fleischer, welcher Hunde,

rats. He has many customers, but it is amusing to see them sneak¹ into the shop, after carefully looking round to make sure that none of their acquaintances are near. I really think that dogs have some means of communicating with each other, and have discovered that their old friends are seeking² after their lives to devour them, for the humblest of street-curs³ growls when anyone merely looks at him. Figaro has a story that a man was followed for a mile by a pack⁴ of dogs fiercely barking at his heels. At first he could not understand to what their attentions were due, till he remembered that he had eaten a rat for his breakfast. The friend of another journalist, who ate a dog called Fox, says that whenever anyone calls out 'Fox' he feels an irresistible impulse which forces him to jump up. As every Christmas a number of books are published containing stories about dogs as remarkable as they are stale, I recommend to the notice of their authors these two veracious tales.

[1] verstohlen schleichen.
[2] trachten.
[3] Gassenköter.
[4] Meute.

Katzen und Ratten verkauft. Er hat viel Kunden, es ist aber doch köstlich zu sehen, wie sie sich verstohlen in seinen Laden schleichen, nachdem sie sich sorgfältig umgeschaut, um sich zu überzeugen, dass Niemand von ihren Bekannten in der Nähe ist. Ich glaube wirklich die Hunde haben eine Methode, sich miteinander zu verständigen, und haben entdeckt, dass ihre alten Freunde ihnen nach dem Leben trachten, um sie zu verzehren. Der elendste Gassenköter knurrt, wenn man ihn nur ansieht. Der Figaro erzählt, ein Mann sei eine halbe Stunde von einer Meute Hunde verfolgt worden, welche wüthend hinter ihm hergebellt hätten. Anfangs konnte er sich nicht erklären, welchem Umstande er diese Aufmerksamkeit verdankte, bis ihm einfiel, dass er eine Ratte zum Frühstück verzehrt hatte. Der Freund eines anderen Journalisten hatte einen Hund verzehrt, welcher Fuchs hiess, und sagt, so oft jemand Fuchs rufe, fühle er einen unwiderstehlichen Trieb, der ihn nöthige, aufzuspringen. Da jede Weihnachten eine Anzahl solcher Bücher erscheinen, welche ebenso wunderbare als abgedroschene Hundegeschichten enthalten, so mache ich die Verfasser solcher Bücher auf diese beiden Geschichten aufmerksam.

The three sentences are done by your class in a quarter of an hour, after ten minutes or so of talk about some of the constructions, conducted with or without reference to their grammars. The first two sentences are hard, and unless your pupils are good you will probably allow them the dictionary, but you do not allow the grammar. Then you start them upon their prose and call them up individually to have their sentences corrected. This is what you may expect. Half your boys only thought of showing that they must write *wurde* not *war*, and give you *Dann wurde ich gezeigt*, forgetting that *zeigen* requires the dative and that you must use *man* in German. A stray *denn* for *dann* calls forth a rating, but there is only one, you are glad to find. Next two-thirds have written *das Zimmer, welches für mich bestimmt war*, which you stigmatize as correct but dull and unidiomatic, and when you find how many have missed this point you stop the prose and call the general attention to it, reminding them how you told them only yesterday that not only did the German affect the form of expression illustrated by 'the never too much to be regretted Mr Smith' but that they even preferred the expanded form 'the never too much to be regretted and always with respect to be remembered Mr Smith'. A *was* for *welches* sends the offender back to his seat to do a small exercise on *wer* and *welcher* until he is wiser as well as sadder. Or perhaps you spare him seeing the genuine vexation his blunder causes him, for coming to close quarters and striking while the iron is hot you will find, to your surprise perhaps if you have an impression that a schoolboy is a careless creature who has no wish to learn, not that your red ink and verbal ratings produce no effect, but that they are apt to produce too much, and that therefore you should always have one easier sentence to encourage and restore self-respect.

In sentence (2) the first boy probably shows you up *Sie verdienen eine Statue sich in Ehre errichtet zu haben*, which sends a complex shudder through you. You set *in Ehre* right at once, and then descend upon *sich* and lastly on the Infinitive mood which you point out cannot stand because of the change of subject. You do not explain the Subj. *errichte* to this boy; he is on too low a level; but you do to the next who is correct but writes *errichten sollte*, which you accept but make him note the terser form *errichte*.

In sentence (3) most give you *bei uns* correctly and *nicht wahr*, but they all miss the *werden* for *wollen* expressing the assumed certainty in the speaker's mind which leaves the other no choice.

In the next week's sentences you take care to bring in at least one of the constructions most generally missed; for instance you set 'A man so popular could not be refused his request', or 'They insisted on going home: I insisted on their staying'. Each boy when he goes down to his seat writes out a fair copy of his sentences, but it is better, if you have time, to make all of them do them again without any help at all during the last five minutes of the lesson. If any boys do really well you may set them instead of this to make six sentences of the same model, a form of exercise at which you will not find that they excel.

The prose you take home and correct out of school, giving it back and talking it over as soon as you can, and exacting a fair copy except where you remit this, or part of it, as a reward for merit. If you are very sumptuous you may chromograph your fair copy and set it to be learnt, not exactly by heart, but so that it can be reproduced from the English. Though all this takes time yet it is valuable. You will be surprised to find upon scrutiny how frequently the constructions and vocabulary of one piece of prose can be employed for the next, and the limits of patience and interest are reached much sooner than the limit of usefulness. And therefore you cannot be too careful in selecting your piece. I venture to say of this piece, because it is not my own, that anyone, who should be set down to do it, would feel that he would like to be able to do it well, and derive some stimulus from the vivacity of the original, and you will all own that the version is admirable, especially in the last two sentences. It would take too long to point out all the constructions which are illustrated by it. You can see them for yourselves.

To be able to render such a piece as this fairly correctly and without missing some of the opportunities for style is the highest level to which we as a matter of fact bring our boys. If they all did as well as the best, it would, I think, be admitted that the level is a fairly high one. Moreover, as the schools are constituted at present, our highest German sets are mostly on the Modern Side where there are not many who are specially gifted in languages or specially interested in pursuing their study, and they only give three schools a week to German.

Still if the top half of this highest set can be transplanted for six weeks to a spot where they will hear and read and talk nothing but German and will set to work in Prendergastian fashion, I maintain that they will return able to converse, within limits, fluently and accurately and able to read a book with pleasure; and to have brought them within so measurable a distance as six weeks *from* such a result does,

I think, go far to establish the claim which I last week made for the Modern Languages.

In French the high-water mark is higher. The same system of sentences done without help and of continuous Prose is the most successful. There are endless good books of Prose Selections. As in Construing Books, the best are those whose subject-matter is the best chosen; the notes are a matter of less importance.

I should like now to show you some portion of the teaching which can be got out of each page of your construing lessons. I will give you as a preliminary one golden rule.

Always *prepare*, however well you may know the language in general and the book which you are doing in particular. Only so will you make the most of your lesson and temper discursiveness with variety and compactness.

Now let me ask you to read through the following passage:

Mais comment arriver au Capitole tant que les ennemis occuperaient la ville? — Pontius Cominius s'offrit pour cette mission périlleuse. Ce jeune Romain, à force de prudence et d'énergie, parvint à tromper la vigilance des ennemis, et fut assez heureux pour rapporter la nomination de Camille comme dictateur. Mais Pontius, qui avait dû gravir un rocher très-escarpé, avait laissé des traces de son passage. Les herbes couchées et la terre éboulée en plusieurs endroits montrèrent aux Gaulois qu'il y avait un chemin accessible pour conduire au Capitole. Ils se mirent en devoir, au milieu de la nuit, de profiter de cette découverte. Ils étaient sur le point de se rendre maîtres des retranchements, car personne ne les avait entendus, lorsque les oies sacrées que l'on entretenait dans le Capitole, près du temple de Junon, coururent aux Gaulois avec de grands cris et en un instant réveillèrent tous les Romains. — Plutarque fait remarquer que les oies ont l'ouïe très-fine, que celles du Capitole étaient assez mal nourries depuis le siége, et qu'elles s'effrayèrent d'autant plus facilement à l'approche des Gaulois, que la faim les tenait éveillées.

It is taken almost at random from a book with which I am better pleased each time I use it, 'Les Petites Ignorances de la Conversation', by M. Rozan. It has no notes but it is full of history as well as of stray information, it is witty, it is written in good style, and it has just a sufficient number of quotations from older authors to make it serve for you to give a good deal of the history of the language if you care to do so. Also, and this is a merit which all teachers will welcome, it is sufficiently difficult to make exposure probable for the idle boy who, knowing a good deal of French, presumes to neglect his lesson, and to make such exposure certain if you begin by a few questions on the subject-matter. After the translation of each paragraph or sentence you ask questions on the grammar. "*Arriver* is Infinitive: with what exact meaning?" "What instance does your grammar give?" "*Dire que cela est vrai!* is that a similar infinitive?" "Has the English language a similar use?" "Has the German?" "Has the Latin?" *Occuperaient*: "We translate by the English imperfect 'were in possession of', but it is Conditional. Which is the more accurate logically?" "Give another instance where French pays more attention to tense than English." *Ville* gives you an opportunity for a remark on the pronunciation of *ll*. *Jeune Romain* suggests the question why *Romain* is here written with a capital letter. *À force de* you call attention to as a turn to be noted, illustrating by the English 'by dint of', and you will ask this next lesson to see who has stored it up, or next minute of the idler in the far corner, or of the eager but inattentive boy who turned on to a new page when you paused to question. *Parvint à:* "Could you say also *réussit à?*" "Yes." "Could you say *succéda à?*" "No." "Then why did you write *succéder* for 'to succeed in an undertaking' in your last exercise, which you will receive back shortly duly underlined, and what does *succéder à* mean?" *Ennemi:* Note the spelling and the pronunciation, and per contra *ennui*.

Pour *rapporter* is also noted. *Avait dû* introduces the whole subject of the compound tenses of the verbs of mood and the special distinction between English on the one hand and French, German, Latin, on the other; and you ask your pet sentences with varied success.

Endroits suggests a caution as to the use of the French *place* which had proved a pitfall in your last exercise. *Gaulois* is distinguished from *Gallois*; *profiter de* is noted for vocabulary, as are *mirent en devoir* and *éboulée*. *Retranchement* = 'entrenchment' suggests a few other instances of words which are like yet different in French and English, e.g. *explication* 'explanation'. *Les avait entendus* gives opportunity if the Form need it for drill in the participle rules, and *de grands cris* similarly brings up the syntax of the article, and *fait remarquer* leads up to a question or two on the construction with *faire*. "Why has *l'ouïe* the *definite* article?" "And can you give me the names of the four other senses?" This you make a general question and suggest that they write in their note-books in parallel columns the senses in French and Latin and German, pointing out that the French words are directly derived from the Latin. Little natural groupings of words such as this are easily remembered. *Celles* enables you to enforce the construction of *celui* on the backward boys; *mal* similarly reminds them of *pis* and *moins*, and other traps for the unwary. *D'autant...que* is a useful construction, often misconstrued, and you are glad to have an instance of it, and the lesson ends with an article which calls for comment, and another past participle. You do not of course dwell at length on all of these points, which are of very various importance and various level: you make your selection. But what I have said may serve to convince you that so far from your French construing books being deficient in matter for teaching, they are too full.

One more hint and I will pass on. You will find in French almost inevitably that for some of your boys the lesson is too easy. You can employ their time to good purpose by exacting from them a written list of idioms from the lesson, or properly classified examples of certain syntax rules, and so show them that there is more to be learnt from a few pages of French than is involved in the rapid acquisition of their meaning. You can also, if you prefer it, make them do a Philological exercise on a portion of the lesson; and this brings us to the consideration of the place which the Historical Study of Modern Languages should occupy. I have not time to discuss the question as fully as its importance deserves, and I must be content to do little more than state my own conclusions. In the first place let me remind you that philology, though as a science it is advancing, is also becoming much more difficult, so much so that many good teachers are beginning to doubt the wisdom of teaching it in the schools at all. In the next place, I would insist upon the importance of distinguishing between Mediaeval and Modern Languages, and of recognising that if your time is limited, what is given to philology is lost to literature. On the other hand, the development of French, so far as derived from Latin, is so clear, and the sound-changes so certainly traceable through the various stages of the literature, and the sound-changes also exhibited by German and English so obvious within certain limits, and the whole subject of derivations so interesting as an accessory of language lessons, that I hope we shall always find time for a certain amount of philology. Again, if more of our classical scholars study French and German seriously, for them philology is more natural and useful, nor is it a slight gain if we can show to all boys how language, treated thus, affords evidence to the student of the history of primitive ages, and takes up the tale where written records begin to fail.

I would not forego the chance of inspiring even one pupil to take up as his life-work the science of language. By these considerations on the one side and the other, I would have you steer your course in this matter. But I would warn you that it is your duty to consider what it is that your pupils want most, and that if the choice lies between Mediaeval French and a third Modern Language, say Italian or Spanish, for nine-tenths of them you ought in all probability to choose the Modern Language, and if your pupils do not learn Latin, you had better leave philology alone.

As a matter of practice I do personally always introduce a little philology into my French lessons, and as an introduction to the subject I say to them, 'French is only bad Latin badly pronounced', and point out by the way what a wonderful thing human speech must be, since by so barbarous a process has been perfected an instrument so delicate and beautiful as French is in the hands of a great writer. And I always use an illustration which I owe to Professor Freeman in order to drive this nail home. I write up on the board these three sentences :

    Habeo bonum equum.
   Ego habeo unum bellum caballum.
    J'ai un beau cheval.

The first is what Cicero said, the second is what his groom said, and the third is elegant modern French. If you seriously teach the subject, what book can be more delightful than 'Brachet's Historical Grammar'? Even if you do not teach it seriously, you can teach orally and illustrate the three main principles, (1) the persistence of the Latin accent, (2) the elision of the medial consonant, (3) the elision of the short medial vowel; and for the rest you will choose in each lesson a few words illustrating the phonetic changes. If you have a list of these properly grouped, your pupils soon begin to detect derivations for themselves, and then you may, if you please, give them Grimm's Law, which is generally, as I think most mistakenly, placed in the forefront of the subject. The small print in Messrs Hachette's 'Public School French Grammar' is perhaps even better than the book mentioned above. Brachet's Etymological French Dictionary you will of course possess.

Verse and Metre.

In German this is so like English that you only need good reading to accustom the ear to detect the rhythm. In French it is otherwise, but I am quite sure that it is worth while to give all boys the elements, because without them French poetry has to English ears no beauty of sound at all. The subject has been done and, it seems to me, done once for all, by Mr Gossett in his 'Manual of French Prosody', a scholarly and excellent book that cannot be praised too highly. Teach your boys how to scan a French Alexandrian—point out to them the metre of a few lyrics, and you will have changed the whole aspect of poetry for them. They may then be in a fair way to appreciate the master-pieces of so marvellous a poet, considered merely as a metrist, as Victor Hugo.

Dictation and Audition.

I regard dictation as very useful from the first. Consider this point only—there is no form of lesson in which it is so easy to keep the attention of every boy continuously at full stretch. You must not of course make your dictation too hard. Five minutes at the end of a school, and three minutes for your boys to correct it—for you will generally take a piece of the book the boys are doing in order that they may turn at once and see what is right—will give you as much practice as you will probably find time for. But it teaches them a great deal. There is a good collection used by French teachers called 'Dictées de l'Hôtel de Ville'. Do not be afraid that your own imperfect pronunciation will spoil the lesson. It might be better, no doubt; but you will find as a matter of fact that the boys who know French fairly well and have heard it spoken will follow you most easily, and that all will steadily improve.

Audition is distinct from this. You can teach it by simply reading over a piece and making your boys give you either *viva voce* or on paper the meaning of it. This also is very valuable. If you have the luck to have a boy who can really pronounce well, set him to read part of the lesson out to your Form—this will be the best way of teaching pronunciation. I promised to say a few more words about this subject. I have said that I think we ought to use phonetic spellings of French words much more than we do, and I think we ought to make a careful selection of the words which are really hard to pronounce. Spend a great deal of time over a few sounds, and you will find that if you can get them really well reproduced—whether in French or German—you have almost done all you want. I have often thought too that it would be possible for a teacher with a good ear to teach pronunciation as a music master teaches singing. Let your boys altogether, or half the class together, declaim a piece of repetition and trust to your power of picking out those boys who are not saying it as they ought. If this could be done the gain would be very great. The objection that we all make, and quite rightly, to pronunciation and elocution lessons is this, that while you are attending to the one boy in teaching him, the others naturally cannot attend; it is too dull. This is not true of construing, but it is true of pronunciation lessons. There is something to be said however for the opinion of Mr Julian Hawthorne expressed in his 'Saxon Studies', when he says that he does not desire to speak German like a native. He could do so, but he will not. He desires to speak it like an Englishman who can use the German instrument of speech. This is not a counsel of perfection, but it will be admitted that it saves a good deal of trouble. Frenchmen smile if you ask them whether so and so does not speak almost like a native, but they always add that *good* English-French is not displeasing to them. French is however certainly harder than German, and I have known not a few Englishmen to whom the flattering question has been addressed, "Aus welchem Theil Deutschlands sind Sie, mein Herr"? But as for the great majority of us, if we are ever mistaken for Frenchmen or Germans at all, it is by our more ignorant fellow-countrymen!

I have left untouched the question how far a knowledge

of Latin can be made to help the study of French, and how far German can be taught by means of the study of the correspondences and differences between it and English. A good knowledge of Latin is a very great aid indeed not only to the acquisition of the meaning of words in French, but also to a thorough knowledge of the grammar. But the kind of knowledge of Latin possessed by the ordinary French pupil is chiefly useful as affording variety and interest to your comments and illustrations, and because in learning Latin grammar boys learn something of grammatical analysis, even if, as is too often the case, they know little more than the nomenclature. I believe myself that this initiation into Grammar would be best done by sensible teaching of English grammar at a somewhat early age, and that the teaching of Latin, French, and all languages would gain if this method were adopted; but the question is too long for me to enter upon now.

Nor have I said anything about Examinations except to acknowledge that they are necessary evils. In the later years of a boy's school life the orderly progress of his study is apt to be exchanged for a hasty attempt to bring his knowledge up to a forced level. Ragged knowledge is dealt with severely by all systems of numerical marking, and yet such raggedness is the natural condition of progress unless we proceed by the most rigorous memory methods. But when you are thus compelled to frame your teaching so as to enable your boys to answer as many as possible of the questions which are likely to be set, I advise you not to make them learn lists of exceptions and vocabularies but to run them through and through carefully set papers which you will look over carefully and make them correct by reference to a large grammar, and to let them do a great deal of paper work in general. And here, though I have said more than once that to discuss text-books would need another lecture, I may be allowed to commend the series of Unseen Passages in French and German and the Sets of Examination Papers lately published by Messrs Rivingtons. I do not desire anything better, and we who have long had to print, chromograph, lithograph or dictate our answers and our papers, may well envy the younger generation of teachers who find all this done for them cheaply and thoroughly.

And here I must stop. I warned you that I was going to plunge into detail, and I fear that I have made the subject seem very dull. But it is not dull. The fault is mine. I have tried to teach a good many subjects, like most of my kind, but the teaching which upon the whole I enjoy most is that of Modern Languages. We need teachers of Modern Languages in the Public Schools, and I believe that the demand will increase. We need especially teachers who to proficiency in Mathematics or Science have added a sound knowledge of one or two Modern Languages. For Mathematical and Science teachers the Schools have long looked to Cambridge; why should they not seek thence their Modern Language Teachers also?

www.ingramcontent.com/pod-product-compliance
Lightning Source LLC
Chambersburg PA
CBHW020300090426
42735CB00009B/1155